W9-CPJ-020

# Celebrate the Holidays

## Create Holiday Magic with **ALDI**® Recipes and Crafts

Visit us at
www.ALDI.com

**Copyright © 2006 Publications International, Ltd.**
All rights reserved. This publication may not be reproduced or quoted in whole or in part by any means whatsoever without written permission from:

Louis Weber, CEO
Publications International, Ltd.
7373 North Cicero Avenue
Lincolnwood, IL 60712

Permission is never granted for commercial purposes.

Distributed by **ALDI®** Inc.
Batavia, IL 60510-1477

Burlwood®, Winking Owl Vineyards® and Wyalla Cove® are registered trademarks of E. & J. Gallo Winery Corporation.

Butterball® is a registered trademark of ConAgra Foods, Inc.

Some of the products listed in this publication may be in limited distribution or only available seasonally.

**Pictured on the front cover** *(clockwise from top left):* Chocolate Gingerbread Cookies *(page 88),* Festive Cranberry Mold *(page 22)* and Roast Turkey with Sausage and Cornbread Stuffing *(page 44).*

**Pictured on the back cover** *(clockwise from top left):* Chocolate Cream-Filled Cake Roll *(page 72),* Chocolate Marble and Praline Cheesecake *(page 68)* and Holiday Pork Crown Roast with Apple Pecan Stuffing and Gravy *(page 46).*

Photography on page 47 by Chris Cassidy Photography, Inc.

Ingredient photography by Al MacDonald Partners LLC.

**Craft Designers and Photographers:** Lucie Sinkler, Silver Lining Digital, Inc. *(page 14);* Phyllis Dunstan, PDR Productions, Inc. *(page 21);* Nancy Wall Hopkins, Sam Griffith Photography *(page 30);* Ed Smith, AIFD, Silver Lining Digital, Inc. *(pages 56 and 87);* Phyllis Dunstan, Silver Lining Digital, Inc. *(page 74);* and Lisa Galvin, Silver Lining Digital, Inc. *(page 93).*

ISBN-13: 978-1-4127-2525-5
ISBN-10: 1-4127-2525-9

Manufactured in U.S.A.

8 7 6 5 4 3 2 1

**Microwave Cooking:** Microwave ovens vary in wattage. Use the cooking times as guidelines and check for doneness before adding more time.

# Table of Contents

## Crafts

**ALDI**® specializes in a select assortment of high-quality, private label products at the lowest possible prices. Quality, taste and satisfaction are always DOUBLE* guaranteed at **ALDI**®. We're so confident about the quality of our products that we guarantee you'll be satisfied too!

*Excludes non-food special purchase items and alcohol.

Quality DOUBLE Guarantee

# CHAPTER 1

# Festive Starters

## Happy Farms® Cheesy Christmas Trees

½ cup Burman's® mayonnaise
1 tablespoon dry ranch salad dressing mix
1 cup (about 4 ounces) Happy Farms® shredded mild Cheddar cheese
¼ cup Reggano® 100% grated Parmesan cheese
12 slices L'oven Fresh® white bread
¼ cup small red bell pepper strips
¼ cup small green bell pepper strips

1. Preheat broiler. Combine mayonnaise and salad dressing mix in medium bowl. Add cheeses; mix well.

2. Toast bread slices; cut into Christmas tree shapes using large cookie cutter.

3. Spread each tree with about 1 tablespoon mayonnaise mixture. Decorate with red and green bell pepper strips. Place on baking sheet. Broil 4 inches from heat 2 to 3 minutes or until bubbling. Serve warm.

*Makes 12 appetizers*

# Happy Farms® Holiday Cheese Tree

**2 cups (about 8 ounces) Happy Farms® finely shredded sharp Cheddar cheese**
**1 package (8 ounces) Happy Farms® cream cheese, softened**
**3 tablespoons finely chopped onion**
**3 tablespoons finely chopped red bell pepper**
**1 tablespoon Nature's Nectar® lemon juice**
**2 teaspoons Worcestershire sauce**
**¾ cup chopped fresh parsley**
   **Yellow bell pepper**
   **Cherry tomatoes, halved**
   **Orange peel twists (optional)**
   **Cambridge® gourmet crackers**
   **Cambridge® snack crackers**

1. Combine Cheddar cheese, cream cheese, onion, red bell pepper, lemon juice and Worcestershire sauce in medium bowl; stir until well blended. Shape into 6-inch-tall cone shape on serving plate. (Cheese tree can be covered and refrigerated up to 8 hours at this stage.)

2. Just before serving press parsley evenly onto cheese tree. Cut yellow bell pepper into desired shapes using cookie cutters or sharp knife. Decorate tree with bell pepper shapes, tomatoes and orange twists. Serve with crackers.

*Makes about 5 cups spread (14 to 16 appetizer servings)*

# Gingerbread Caramel Corn

**2 packages Corn Town® microwave popcorn**
**1 cup Southern Grove® cashew halves**
**1 cup Sweet Harvest® packed light brown sugar**
**½ cup (1 stick) Happy Farms® butter**
**¼ cup Baker's Corner light corn syrup**
**1 teaspoon ground ginger**
**1 teaspoon ground cinnamon**
**½ teaspoon Baker's Corner® baking soda**

1. Preheat oven to 250°F. Line 17×11-inch shallow roasting pan with Kwik-N-Fresh® aluminum foil or use disposable foil roasting pan. Pop corn; measure 10 cups. Combine popcorn and cashews in prepared pan; set aside.

2. Combine brown sugar, butter and corn syrup in heavy 1½- or 2-quart saucepan. Bring to a boil over medium heat, stirring constantly. Wash down* sugar crystals with pastry brush, if necessary. Attach candy thermometer to side of pan, making sure bulb is submerged in sugar mixture but not touching bottom of pan. Continue boiling, without stirring, about 5 minutes or until sugar mixture reaches soft-crack stage (290°F) on candy thermometer. Remove from heat; stir in ginger, cinnamon and baking soda.

3. Immediately drizzle sugar mixture slowly over popcorn mixture; stir until evenly coated. Bake 1 hour, stirring quickly every 15 minutes.

4. Meanwhile line baking sheet with Kwik-N-Fresh® aluminum foil. Transfer caramel corn to prepared baking sheet; spread in single layer. Cool completely, about 10 minutes. Store in airtight container at room temperature.                    *Makes about 10 cups*

*\*To wash down the crystals from the side of a pan, use a pastry brush dipped in hot water. Gently brush the crystals down into the syrup or collect them on the brush bristles. Dip the brush frequently in hot water to clean off the bristles.*

# Antipasto Crescent Bites

**4 ounces (½ package) Happy Farms® cream cheese**
**2 Goldhen® eggs**
**2 tablespoons water**
**2 packages (8 ounces each) Buehler's® refrigerated crescent rolls**
**8 (3×¾-inch) strips roasted red pepper**
**8 Grandessa® artichoke quarters, drained**
**2 thin slices Deli Premium salami or pepperoni, each cut into 4 strips**
**8 Diomede® stuffed Spanish olives, cut into halves**

1. Preheat oven to 375°F. Cut cream cheese into 32 equal pieces, about 1 teaspoon per piece; set aside.

2. Combine eggs and water; mix well. Remove crescent roll dough from packages. Unroll on lightly floured surface. Cut each dough triangle in half to form 2 triangles. Brush edges of triangles lightly with egg mixture.

3. Prepare Fillings (recipes follow). Place fillings one at a time on dough triangle; fold over and pinch edges to seal. Place filled triangles evenly spaced on ungreased baking sheet. Brush with egg mixture.

4. Bake 12 to 14 minutes or until golden brown. Serve warm.                  *Makes 32 pieces*

Red Pepper Cheese Filling: Wrap 1 red pepper strip around 1 piece cream cheese. Repeat seven times.

Artichoke Cheese Filling: Press 1 quarter artichoke heart into 1 piece cream cheese. Repeat seven times.

Salami Cheese Filling: Wrap 1 salami strip around 1 piece cream cheese. Repeat seven times.

Olive Cheese Filling: Press 2 olive halves into 1 piece cream cheese. Repeat seven times.

Prepare Ahead: Bites may be made ahead. Cool and store in an airtight container in the refrigerator. To serve, reheat on baking sheet in preheated 325°F oven 7 to 8 minutes or until warmed through. Do not microwave.

# Holiday Citrus Punch

### Ingredients

**2 cups (16 ounces) Belmont French vanilla ice cream, softened**
**Fresh or frozen raspberries**
**2 cups Nature's Nectar® cranberry apple juice**
**2 cups Nature's Nectar® ruby red grapefruit juice**
**1 can (12 ounces) frozen lemonade concentrate, thawed**
**1 cup cold water**
**¼ cup fresh lime juice**
**1 bottle (2 liters) Sweet Valley® Citro Zip soda, chilled**

### Supplies

**Parchment paper**
**Assorted cookie cutters in star, snowflake or holiday shapes**

1. Line 9-inch square baking dish with parchment paper. Spread ice cream evenly in prepared dish; freeze until firm. Meanwhile, place baking sheet in freezer to chill.

2. Remove ice cream from baking dish. Using open-style cookie cutters, cut out desired shapes from frozen ice cream. Carefully transfer cutouts to chilled baking sheet. Press raspberry into center of each cutout. Cover; freeze until ready to serve.

3. Combine cranberry apple juice, grapefruit juice, lemonade, water and lime juice in punch bowl. Add soda just before serving. Carefully float ice cream cutouts in punch.

*Makes 24 to 26 servings*

### HOLIDAY TIP

*If you're in a hurry to make punch, just float scoops of Belmont ice cream in the punch instead of making cutouts.* **ALDI®** *carries a wide variety of fruit juices—apple, grape, lemon, cranberry and citrus. Mix up your favorite flavors and top with ice cream for a popular punch to please all ages.*

# Parmesan Ranch Snack Mix

1½ cups Millville® corn cereal squares
1½ cups Millville® rice cereal squares
2 cups Cambridge® oyster crackers
1 package (5 ounces) bagel chips, broken in half
2 to 3 cups Clancy's® mini twist pretzels
1 cup shelled Southern Grove® deluxe pistachio nuts
2 tablespoons Reggano® 100% grated Parmesan cheese
¼ cup (½ stick) Happy Farms® butter, melted
1 package (1 ounce) dry ranch salad dressing mix
½ teaspoon Spice Club® garlic powder

## Slow Cooker Directions

1. Combine cereal, oyster crackers, bagel chips, pretzels, nuts and Parmesan cheese in slow cooker; mix gently. Combine butter, salad dressing mix and garlic powder in small bowl. Pour over cereal mixture; toss lightly to coat. Cover; cook on LOW 3 hours.

2. Remove cover; stir gently. Cook, uncovered, 30 minutes to crisp.

*Makes about 9¹⁄₂ cups snack mix*

# Festive Bacon and Cheese Dip

2 packages (8 ounces each) Happy Farms® cream cheese, cut into cubes
2 packages (8 ounces each) Happy Farms® Colby cheese, cut into cubes
1 cup Friendly Farms half & half
2 tablespoons Briargate® yellow mustard
1 tablespoon minced onion
2 teaspoons Worcestershire sauce
½ teaspoon Sebree® salt
¼ teaspoon Kahlner's® red pepper sauce
1 pound Roseland® bacon, crisp-cooked and crumbled
Casa Mamita® white round tortilla chips
Assorted raw vegetables, cut into small pieces

## Slow Cooker Directions

1. Combine cream cheese, Colby cheese, half & half, mustard, onion, Worcestershire sauce, salt and pepper sauce in 1¹⁄₂-quart slow cooker. Cover; cook, stirring occasionally, on LOW 1 hour or until cheese melts.

2. Stir in bacon; adjust seasonings. Keep warm in slow cooker, stirring occasionally. Serve with tortilla chips and vegetables. *Makes about 4 cups dip*

# Hot Buttered Cider

²⁄₃ **cup Sweet Harvest® packed brown sugar**
½ **cup (1 stick) Happy Farms® butter, softened**
½ **cup Golden Nectar® honey**
½ **teaspoon ground cinnamon**
½ **teaspoon ground nutmeg**
 1 **bottle (128 ounces) Nature's Nectar apple cider**

1. Beat brown sugar, butter, honey, cinnamon and nutmeg until well blended and fluffy. Place butter mixture in tightly covered container. Refrigerate up to 2 weeks. Bring butter mixture to room temperature before using.

2. To serve, heat apple cider in large saucepan over medium heat until hot. Fill each mug with hot apple cider; stir in 1 tablespoon butter mixture per 1 cup cider.

*Makes 12 to 16 servings*

## See-Through Surprise Gift Bag

### supplies

- 12×45 inches velvet or other fabric
- Ruler
- Pencil
- Scissors
- 7×5 inches organdy
- Straight pins
- Sewing machine
- Thread to match
- 2 yards decorative ribbon, ¼ to ½ inch wide
- Needle
- 4 large decorative beads

1. Cut two 8½×9½-inch rectangles from main fabric. Make "window" in 1 fabric piece by cutting 3×4-inch rectangle in center. On wrong side of fabric, cover opening with organdy; pin in place. With right side up, sew organdy to fabric along cut edge. Baste decorative ribbon around organdy window to cover seam. Sew in place. Remove basting stitches.

2. With right sides facing, pin and then stitch sides and bottom of fabric pieces together. Fold bottom corners flat. Sew a line across about ¾ inch from corner edge. Turn inside out.

3. Sew ribbon along top of bag, then fold it over to inside of bag opening. Hand-sew other edge of ribbon in place.

4. To make handles, cut four 7-inch lengths of ribbon. Place 2 lengths on top of each other, and sew along edges. Repeat for other 2 lengths. Slip 2 beads on each handle. Pin handles to bag opening. Sew in place.

# Herb Cheese Twists

**2 tablespoons Happy Farms® butter**
**¼ cup Reggano® 100% grated Parmesan cheese**
**1 teaspoon dried basil**
**¼ teaspoon Spice Club® garlic powder**
**1 can (7½ ounces) Buehler's® refrigerated buttermilk biscuits**

1. Preheat oven to 400°F. Microwave butter in small microwavable bowl on MEDIUM (50%) just until melted; cool slightly. Stir in cheese, basil and garlic powder; set aside.

2. Pat each biscuit into 5×2-inch rectangle. Spread 1 teaspoon butter mixture onto each rectangle. Cut each in half lengthwise. Twist each strip 4 or 5 times. Place on prepared baking sheet. Bake 8 to 10 minutes or until golden brown.     *Makes 20 twists*

# Shrimp Spread

**2 cups (10 ounces) Sea Queen® deluxe cooked medium shrimp**
**1 package (8 ounces) Happy Farms® cream cheese, softened**
**¼ cup (½ stick) Happy Farms® butter, softened**
**2 tablespoons Burman's® mayonnaise**
**2 tablespoons Sea Queen cocktail sauce**
**1 tablespoon Nature's Nectar® lemon juice**
**½ teaspoon Kahlner's® red pepper sauce**
**1 tablespoon chopped fresh parsley**
**Cambridge® entertainment crackers**
**Assorted raw vegetables**

1. Thaw shrimp according to package directions. Cut off shrimp tails. Finely chop shrimp.

2. Blend cream cheese, butter, mayonnaise, cocktail sauce, lemon juice and pepper sauce in large bowl until smooth. Fold shrimp and parsley into cream cheese mixture.

3. Pack spread into decorative serving crock or mold lined with Kwik-N-Fresh® plastic wrap. Cover; refrigerate overnight. Serve spread in crock or invert mold onto serving platter and remove plastic wrap. Serve with crackers and raw vegetables.

*Makes 2¹/₂ cups*

# Banana Nog

**2 cups Friendly Farms® milk**
**2 ripe bananas, cut into pieces**
**½ cup Sweet Harvest® granulated sugar**
**2 Goldhen® egg yolks**
**⅓ to ⅔ cup light rum**
**¼ cup crème de cacao or chocolate-flavored liqueur (optional)**
**1 teaspoon Spice Club pure vanilla**
**2 cups Friendly Farms half & half, chilled**
    **Friendly Farms aerosol whipped cream**
    **Baker's Corner baking cocoa**

1. Place milk, banana and sugar in blender or food processor; process until smooth. Place milk mixture in medium saucepan. Heat to simmering over medium heat, stirring occasionally.

2. Lightly beat egg yolks in small bowl; whisk about ½ cup milk mixture into egg yolks. Whisk yolk mixture back into saucepan. Cook over medium heat, stirring constantly, until thick enough to coat the back of a spoon. *Do not boil.*

3. Remove from heat; stir in rum, crème de cacao, if desired, and vanilla. Pour into large heatproof pitcher or bowl. Cover; refrigerate until chilled.

4. Just before serving, stir half & half into eggnog mixture. Serve in mugs or punch cups; garnish with whipped cream and sifted cocoa.                    *Makes 6 to 8 servings*

# Holiday Wine Punch

**Grape Ice Ring (recipe follows)**
**½ cup Sweet Harvest® granulated sugar**
**½ cup water**
**1 bottle (750 ml) Burlwood® merlot wine, chilled**
**2 cups white grape juice, chilled**
**1 cup peach schnapps, chilled**

1. Prepare Grape Ice Ring.

2. Combine sugar and water in small saucepan. Bring to a boil. Boil, stirring constantly, until sugar dissolves. Cool to room temperature. Cover; refrigerate until chilled, about 2 hours.

3. Combine wine, grape juice, schnapps and sugar syrup in punch bowl just before serving. Float Grape Ice Ring in punch.                    *Makes 14 servings*

# Grape Ice Ring

**2 pounds assorted seedless grapes (Thompson, Red Empress, etc.)**
**Lemon leaves* (optional)**

*\*These nontoxic leaves are available in florist shops.*

1. Fill 4-cup ring mold with water to within ³/₄ inch of top. Freeze until firm, about 8 hours or overnight. Arrange clusters of grapes and leaves, if desired, on ice; fill with water to top of mold. Freeze until solid, about 6 hours.

2. To unmold, dip bottom of mold briefly in hot water.                    *Makes 1 ring*

**Wine Tip**

*Burlwood® merlot is a medium-bodied wine with luscious flavors of blueberry and black cherry combined with subtle notes of vanilla and toasty oak. Enjoy Burlwood® merlot in this festive punch and purchase a few extra bottles to serve with your holiday dinner.*

# Mulled Cranberry Tea

**2 Benner® tea bags**
**1 cup boiling water**
**6 cups Nature's Nectar® cranberry juice**
**½ cup Fit & Active® dried cranberries**
**⅓ cup Sweet Harvest® granulated sugar**
**1 large lemon, cut into ¼-inch slices**
**4 cinnamon sticks**
**6 whole cloves**
  **Additional thin lemon slices and cinnamon sticks for garnish**

## Slow Cooker Directions

1. Place tea bags in 3- to 4-quart slow cooker. Pour boiling water over tea bags; cover and let stand 5 minutes. Remove and discard tea bags. Stir in cranberry juice, cranberries, sugar, lemon slices, 4 cinnamon sticks and cloves. Cover; cook on LOW 2 to 3 hours or on HIGH 1 to 2 hours.

2. Remove and discard lemon slices, cinnamon sticks and cloves. Serve in warm mugs with additional fresh lemon slices and cinnamon sticks.          *Makes 8 servings*

# A Mug of Winter Warmth

## supplies

- Tracing paper
- Pencil
- Scissors
- White ceramic mug
- Clear tape
- Grease pencil
- Enamel paint: black, orange, blue, green, red, white
- Paintbrushes
- Paper towel

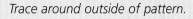

*Trace around outside of pattern.*

1. Trace or photocopy pattern above. Cut out pattern. Tape it to side of mug. Use grease pencil to trace around outside of shape. Remove pattern.

2. From same paper pattern, cut out hat and nose. Tape them on mug. Use grease pencil to trace around pieces. Cut out holly leaves and berries. Trace them on mug. Draw in eyes, mouth and neckline of sweater.

3. Paint hat black, nose orange and sweater blue. Let dry. Paint eyes, nose outline, mouth and face outline black. Let dry.

4. Paint holly leaves green and berries red. Add white to blue paint to make light blue. Paint light blue shadow under brim of hat and light blue vertical stripes on sweater. Use light blue paint to add snowflakes around mug.

5. Add enough water to red paint to make a wash. Use to paint cheek on snowman. Let paint dry thoroughly for several hours.

6. Wipe off any grease pencil marks with damp paper towel. Cure paint according to directions on paint jars.

# CHAPTER 2

# Splendid Sides

## Festive Sweet Harvest® Cranberry Mold

½ cup water
2 packages (3 ounces each) Jell-Rite® strawberry gelatin
1 cup Sweet Harvest® jellied cranberry sauce
1½ cups Nature's Nectar® cranberry juice
1 cup sliced bananas
½ cup Southern Grove® chopped walnuts, toasted*

*To toast walnuts, spread in single layer on baking sheet. Bake in preheated 350°F 5 to 7 minutes or until golden brown, stirring frequently. Or, spread in single layer on plate. Microwave 1 to 2 minutes, stirring every 30 seconds.*

1. Bring water to a boil in medium saucepan over medium-high heat. Add gelatin and stir until dissolved. Fold in cranberry sauce. Reduce heat to medium; cook until sauce is melted. Stir in cranberry juice.

2. Refrigerate mixture until slightly thickened. Fold in banana slices and walnuts. Pour mixture into 4-cup mold. Cover tightly with Kwik-N-Fresh® aluminum foil. Refrigerate at least 4 hours or until gelatin is set. Unmold onto platter.          *Makes 8 servings*

Tip: To easily unmold a gelatin salad, loosen the edges of the mold by running a knife around the edge of the mold. Dip the mold into a large bowl of warm water for about 10 seconds, immersing it almost to the rim. Cover the mold with a serving plate and invert. Give the mold a gentle shake or two. If it does not slide out at once, return it to the bowl of water for a few seconds

# Old-Fashioned Herb Stuffing

**½ cup (1 stick) Happy Farms® butter**
**1 cup chopped onion**
**½ cup sliced celery**
**½ cup chopped carrot**
**1 can (14½ ounces) Chef's Cupboard® chicken broth**
**1¼ cups water**
**1 tablespoon chopped fresh thyme *or* 1 teaspoon dried thyme**
**1 tablespoon chopped fresh sage *or* 1 teaspoon dried sage**
**½ teaspoon paprika**
**½ to 1 teaspoon Spice Club® black pepper**
**2 boxes (6 ounces each) Chef's Cupboard® chicken flavor stuffing mix**

1. Melt butter in large saucepan over medium heat. Add onion, celery and carrot; cover and cook 10 minutes or until vegetables are tender.

2. Add broth, water, thyme, sage, paprika and pepper to saucepan; bring to a simmer. Stir in stuffing; mix well. Remove pan from heat. Cover; let stand 5 minutes. Fluff with fork and serve.

*Makes 8 cups*

Prepare Ahead: Stuffing may be prepared up to 1 day before serving. Coat 1¹/₂-quart baking dish with Ariel® no stick cooking spray. Spoon stuffing into dish. Cover tightly with Kwik-N-Fresh® aluminum foil and store in the refrigerator. Let stand at room temperature 30 minutes before heating. Add a small amount of broth or water, if needed, for additional moisture. Bake in 350°F oven for 20 to 25 minutes or until heated through.

## HOLIDAY TIP

*Buffets make holiday parties easy. Serve appetizers away from the main buffet table to keep guests entertained while you set up the buffet. Set out room temperature and cold foods first. Bring out the hot dishes just before you are ready to eat. Place desserts and coffee in a separate area so that you can clean the main table quickly and get back to the party.*

# Glazed Maple Acorn Squash

**1 large acorn or golden acorn squash**
**¼ cup water**
**2 tablespoons Aunt Maple's® pancake syrup**
**1 tablespoon Happy Farms® butter, melted**
**¼ teaspoon ground cinnamon**

1. Preheat oven to 375°F.

2. Cut stem and blossom ends from squash. Cut squash crosswise into 4 or 5 equal slices. Discard seeds and membrane. Place water in 13×9-inch baking dish. Arrange squash in dish; cover with Kwik-N-Fresh® aluminum foil. Bake 30 minutes or until squash is tender.

3. Combine syrup, butter and cinnamon in small bowl. Uncover squash; pour off water. Brush squash with syrup mixture, letting excess pool in center of squash. Return to oven; bake 10 minutes or until syrup mixture is bubbly.

*Makes 4 or 5 servings*

## HOLIDAY TIP

*Softening squash can make slicing it much easier. Pierce the rind in a few places to allow steam to escape. Place the squash in the microwave and heat on HIGH 1 to 2 minutes. Let it stand about 3 minutes and then slice as the recipe directs.*

# Delicious Corn Soufflé

**3 Goldhen® eggs**
**3 tablespoons Grandma's Best® all-purpose flour**
**1 tablespoon Sweet Harvest® granulated sugar**
**½ teaspoon Spice Club® black pepper**
**2 cups Happy Harvest® frozen whole kernel corn,**
    **thawed and drained**
**1 can (14¾ ounces) Happy Harvest® cream style corn**
**1 cup (about 4 ounces) Happy Farms® finely shredded Mexican style**
    **cheese or Colby & Monterey Jack cheese**
**1 jar (2 ounces) chopped pimientos, drained**
**⅓ cup Friendly Farms® milk**

1. Preheat oven to 350°F. Spray 8-inch round baking dish with Ariel® no stick cooking spray. Place dish in oven.

2. Combine eggs, flour, sugar and pepper in large bowl; beat with electric mixer at high speed until smooth. Stir in corn kernels, cream corn, cheese, pimientos and milk. Pour into hot baking dish. Bake, uncovered, 55 minutes or until set. Let stand 15 minutes before serving.     *Makes 6 servings*

# Happy Harvest® Mashed Sweet Potatoes with Caramelized Pineapple

**2 cans (15 ounces each) Happy Harvest® cut sweet potatoes, drained**
**⅓ cup Nature's Nectar® 100% pure Florida orange juice**
**1 Goldhen® egg**
**2 tablespoons Happy Farms® butter, softened**
**½ teaspoon Sebree® salt**
**¼ teaspoon Spice Club® black pepper**
**1 can Sweet Harvest® pineapple chunks, drained**
**¼ cup Sweet Harvest® packed brown sugar**

1. Preheat oven to 350°F. Butter 1-quart baking dish.

2. Place sweet potatoes in large bowl; mash. Add orange juice, egg, butter, salt and pepper; mix well. Place potato mixture in prepared baking dish. Arrange pineapple on top; sprinkle with brown sugar. Cover tightly with Kwik-N-Fresh® aluminum foil. Bake 20 minutes. Remove cover; bake 20 minutes or until sugar is caramelized. Serve immediately.     *Makes 6 servings*

# Honey Cranberry Sauce

**3 cups fresh cranberries**
**1 can (20 ounces) Sweet Harvest® crushed pineapple in juice**
**½ cup Golden Nectar® honey**
**¼ cup Sweet Harvest® granulated sugar**
**¼ cup Sweet Harvest® premium golden raisins**
**2 tablespoons water**
**½ teaspoon ground allspice**
**⅛ teaspoon Sebree® salt**

1. Combine cranberries, pineapple with juice, honey, sugar, raisins, water, allspice and salt in large saucepan. Bring to a boil over medium-high heat. Reduce heat to medium. Cook, uncovered, 5 to 6 minutes or until cranberries pop.

2. Cook 5 to 10 minutes or until mixture boils and thickens. Transfer to serving bowl. Serve warm or chilled.

*Makes 4 cups sauce*

## O Christmas Tree

### supplies

- Flat-topped 1½-quart glass or acrylic jar
- Food gift
- One 6- to 8-inch miniature artificial Christmas tree
- Hot glue gun and glue sticks or all-purpose craft glue
- 2 to 3 miniature holiday gifts
- Miniature tree decorations (star, lights, ornaments, garlands)
- Green floral wire
- 1 yard of 2½-inch-wide Christmas ribbon

1. Fill the jar with the food gift as desired. Close the jar. Center the tree on top of the lid and attach with the hot glue gun or craft glue. Let dry.

2. Glue the gifts under the tree as desired. Let dry. Decorate the tree as desired, attaching ornaments with floral wire.

3. To make the bow, circle the ribbon around the lid. Tie the ends into a loose knot. Trim the ends as desired.

# Sweet Harvest® Spicy Pumpkin Soup

**1 can (4 ounces) diced green chiles, drained**
**¼ cup Friendly Farms sour cream**
**¼ cup fresh cilantro leaves**
**1 can (15 ounces) Sweet Harvest® solid pack pumpkin**
**1 can (14½ ounces) Chef's Cupboard® chicken broth**
**½ cup water**
**¼ teaspoon Sebree® salt**
**½ teaspoon ground cumin**
**½ teaspoon chili powder**
**¼ teaspoon Spice Club® garlic powder**
**⅛ teaspoon ground red pepper (optional)**
**    Additional Friendly Farms sour cream (optional)**

1. Combine chiles, ¼ cup sour cream and cilantro in mini food processor or blender; process until smooth.

2. Combine pumpkin, broth, water, salt, cumin, chili powder, garlic powder and red pepper, if desired, in large saucepan. Stir in ¼ cup green chile mixture. Bring to a boil; reduce heat to medium. Simmer, uncovered, 5 minutes, stirring occasionally.

3. Pour into serving bowls. Top each serving with small dollops of remaining green chile mixture and additional sour cream, if desired. Run tip of spoon through dollops to swirl.

*Makes 4 servings*

# Holiday Green Salad with Pears and Pecans

¼ cup Burman's® mayonnaise
¼ cup Friendly Farms sour cream
1 tablespoon finely minced onion
1 tablespoon Carlini® extra virgin olive oil
2 teaspoons balsamic vinegar
⅛ teaspoon Spice Club® black pepper
   Sebree® salt to taste
1 bag (10 ounces) Freshire Farms® Italian salad blend
2 ripe pears or apples, cored and thinly sliced
1 cup (about 4 ounces) Happy Farms® finely shredded sharp Cheddar cheese
½ cup Southern Grove® pecan halves, toasted* and coarsely chopped
   Pomegranate seeds (optional)

*To toast pecans, spread in single layer on baking sheet. Bake in preheated 350°F 5 to 7 minutes or until golden brown, stirring frequently. Or, spread in single layer on plate. Microwave 1 to 2 minutes, stirring every 30 seconds.*

1. Combine mayonnaise, sour cream, onion, oil, vinegar, pepper and salt in small bowl. Blend well; set aside.

2. Arrange greens evenly on four plates. Place pear slices around edges of plates. Sprinkle cheese and pecans over greens. Drizzle dressing evenly over salads. Garnish with pomegranate seeds.

*Makes 4 servings*

# Sweet Potato Gratin

**3 pounds sweet potatoes (about 5 large)**
**½ cup (1 stick) Happy Farms® butter, divided**
**¼ cup plus 2 tablespoons Sweet Harvest® packed light brown sugar, divided**
**2 Goldhen® eggs**
**⅔ cup Nature's Nectar® 100% pure Florida orange juice**
**2 teaspoons ground cinnamon, divided**
**½ teaspoon Sebree® salt**
**¼ teaspoon ground nutmeg**
**⅓ cup Grandma's Best® all-purpose flour**
**¼ cup Millville® uncooked quick oats**
**⅓ cup Southern Grove® chopped pecans or walnuts**

1. Bake sweet potatoes about 1 hour or until tender. Or, pierce sweet potatoes several times with fork and place on microwavable plate. Microwave at HIGH 16 to 18 minutes, rotating and turning potatoes over after 9 minutes. Let stand 5 minutes.

2. Preheat oven to 350°F. Spray 1½-quart baking dish or gratin dish with Ariel® no stick cooking spray.

3. Cut hot sweet potatoes lengthwise into halves. Scoop pulp into large bowl. Add ¼ cup butter and 2 tablespoons sugar; beat with electric mixer at medium speed until butter is melted. Add eggs, orange juice, 1½ teaspoons cinnamon, salt and nutmeg. Beat until smooth. Pour mixture into prepared dish; smooth top.

4. For topping, combine flour, oats, remaining ¼ cup sugar and ½ teaspoon cinnamon in medium bowl. Cut in remaining ¼ cup butter until mixture resembles coarse crumbs. Stir in pecans. Sprinkle topping evenly over sweet potatoes.

5. Bake 25 to 30 minutes or until sweet potatoes are heated through. For crisper topping, broil 5 inches from heat 2 to 3 minutes or until golden brown.          *Makes 6 to 8 servings*

Prepare Ahead: After completing step 4, Sweet Potato Gratin may be covered and refrigerated up to 1 day. Let stand at room temperature 1 hour before baking.

# Roasted Potatoes and Pearl Onions

**3 pounds red potatoes, well-scrubbed and cut into 1½-inch cubes**
**1 package (10 ounces) pearl onions, peeled, *or* 4 to 6 small onions,**
    **peeled and quartered**
**2 tablespoons Carlini® extra virgin olive oil**
**2 teaspoons dried basil or dried thyme**
**1 teaspoon paprika**
**¾ teaspoon Sebree® salt**
**¾ teaspoon dried rosemary**
**¾ teaspoon Spice Club® black pepper**

1. Preheat oven to 400°F.

2. Place potatoes and onions in large roasting pan. Do not use glass baking dish or potatoes will not brown. Drizzle with oil. Combine basil, paprika, salt, rosemary and pepper in small bowl; mix well. Sprinkle over potatoes and onions; toss well to coat lightly with oil and seasonings.

3. Bake 20 minutes; toss well. Bake 15 to 20 minutes more or until potatoes are browned and tender. *Makes 8 servings*

# Delicious Butternut Squash Soup

**1 tablespoon Happy Farms® butter**
**1 large onion, coarsely chopped**
**1 tablespoon Spice Club® minced garlic**
**1 medium butternut squash (about 1½ pounds), peeled, seeded**
    **and cut into ½-inch pieces**
**1 medium Granny Smith apple, peeled, cored and cubed**
**2 cans (14½ ounces each) Chef's Cupboard® chicken broth, divided**
**1 tablespoon Sweet Harvest® packed light brown sugar**
**½ teaspoon Sebree® salt**
**½ teaspoon ground or freshly grated nutmeg**
**¼ teaspoon ground cinnamon**
**¼ teaspoon Spice Club® black pepper**
    **Friendly Farms sour cream**
    **Chives (optional)**

1. Melt butter in large saucepan over medium heat. Add onion and garlic; cook and stir 3 minutes. Add squash, apple and 1 can broth; bring to a boil over high heat. Reduce heat to low. Cover; simmer 20 minutes or until squash is very tender.

2. Process squash mixture in small batches in food processor or blender until smooth. Return soup to saucepan; add remaining can of broth, sugar, salt, nutmeg, cinnamon and pepper. Simmer, uncovered, 5 minutes, stirring occasionally.*

3. Ladle soup into soup bowls. Place sour cream in small Kwik-N-Fresh® food storage bag. Cut off tiny corner of bag; drizzle sour cream onto soup in decorative design. Garnish with chives.                  *Makes 6 servings (about 5 cups)*

*\*At this point, soup may be covered and refrigerated up to 2 days before serving. Reheat over medium heat, stirring occasionally.*

Cream of Butternut Squash Soup: Add ½ cup Friendly Farms whipping cream or half & half with the second can of broth. Proceed as directed.

# Celebrate the Season

# DECEMBER

### Season's greetings

To keep family and friends close, send beautiful, handmade greeting cards. Or, purchase cards and personalize them with a family photograph and a holiday newsletter.

**3**

### Decorate with flowers

For instant holiday cheer, decorate with colorful poinsettias. Plant amaryllis or paper white bulbs for dramatic beauty later in the month. Layer pebbles in the bottom of a tall decorative container. Place the bulbs in the pebbles leaving at least ⅓ of the top exposed. Keep watered to just touch the bottom of the bulbs for beautiful blooms in 4 to 6 weeks.

**4**

### Shop online

Check out **www.ALDI.com** for upcoming special purchase items that make terrific gifts at a great price. Then, visit your local **ALDI**® store to purchase the items you saw online. For food gifts, pick up succulent shrimp, decadent European chocolate and many other top quality foods for the holiday.

**5**

**6**

**10**

### Pack and mail holiday gifts

Mail packages to ensure they arrive on time and to avoid expensive express shipping charges. Use sturdy boxes. After adding the gifts, fill the box with crumpled newspaper. Be sure the address and return address are clear and prominently displayed.

**11**

**12**

**13**

**17**

### Shop for entertaining

Discover top-quality products for holiday entertaining at an incredible value at **ALDI**®. You'll find a nice variety of affordable wines for every party. And, don't forget specialty meats, such as whole turkeys and elegant pork crown roasts—perfect for festive holiday meals.

**18**

**19**

**20**

### Cookies for Santa

Have the children put out Chocolate Gingerbread Cookies *(page 88)* and milk for Santa. Stuff the stockings with Choceur® chocolate bars and Chazoo® fruit snacks from **ALDI**®. Don't forget to make stockings for your pets.

**24**

*Merry Christmas*

**25**

### Let it snow

Plan a fun family outing such as a sledding party, a snowman building contest, a skating party or a holiday walk. When they come in from the cold, serve Hot Buttered Cider *(page 14)* and Moist Pumpkin Cookies *(page 92)*—delicious snacks to warm up the crowd.

**26**

**27**

### Share the joy

Take time to look after others. Donate to your favorite charity or help out at a local food pantry. Visit elderly members of your family. And read, play games and sing songs with your kids.

**28**

### Celebrate the New Year!

Whether you're hosting a casual or elegant party, **ALDI**® has everything you'll need to celebrate the New Year. Pick up champagne, shrimp and cocktail sauce, sliced cheeses and ready-to-serve snacks so you can spend more time having fun.

**29**

**30**

HAPPY NEW YEAR

### Make a list and check it twice

Make a master list of everything that needs to be done for the holidays. Decide dates and menus for holiday get-togethers. Make a gift list. Remember **ALDI®** gift certificates are perfect for gift exchanges, grab bags and almost everyone—teachers, the mailman, grandparents and friends.

1

### Family crafting day

Get the family together to create beautiful decorations and gifts that will be cherished for a lifetime. Choose a craft like the Jolly Jingle Bell Candleholder *(page 87)*. Make several at one time for centerpieces or gifts for your favorite holiday hosts.

2

### Stock the pantry

Avoid the rush and stock your pantry early with everything you'll need for the holiday season. **ALDI®** carries a great variety of baking supplies for festive treats and desserts. And don't forget to purchase an extra supply of snacks and sodas for your holiday visitors.

7

8

### Deck the halls!

Get in the holiday spirit with decorations. Bring home a tree, put on your favorite holiday music and light a fire. Bring out special treats such as Gingerbread Caramel Corn *(page 8)*. Your family will have a joyous time decorating for the season.

9

14

### Make holiday treats

Gather family and friends for a fun and festive day making delicious treats. Try Candy Cane Fudge *(page 80)* or Chocolate Surprise Cookies *(page 90)*. Be sure to make double batches for holiday parties and tasty gifts.

15

### Host a cookie swap

Invite 8 friends to each make 8 dozen of their favorite holiday cookies. Then get together and exchange cookies. Serve Grandessa® German roasted coffee and Holiday Citrus Punch *(page 10)*. Each person will go home with 8 dozen cookies—1 dozen of each kind.

16

### Organize gift wrapping supplies

Gather papers, scissors, tape, gift tags, ribbons and gift bags in one place. Clear plastic tubs or containers help to keep supplies together in one organized location.

21

22

### Last minute preparations

Get ready for a fabulous holiday dinner. Pull items out of the freezer to thaw in the refrigerator. Polish the silver. Stop by **ALDI®** for salad greens, eggs, milk and fresh bread. Pick up **ALDI®** gift certificates for last-minute gifts.

23

CHAPTER 3

# Merry Main Dishes

## Appleton® Cranberry-Glazed Ham

**1 Appleton® spiral sliced smoked honey ham half**
   **(about 7 to 8 pounds) with glaze packet**
**¾ cup Sweet Harvest® jellied cranberry sauce**
**¼ cup Briargate® Dijon mustard**
**1 teaspoon ground cinnamon**
**¼ teaspoon ground allspice**

1. Preheat oven to 325°F. Remove glaze packet from ham; set aside. Line shallow roasting pan with Kwik-N-Fresh® aluminum foil.

2. Place ham face down in prepared pan. Combine cranberry sauce, mustard, cinnamon, allspice and contents of glaze packet; mix well. Spread $1/3$ cup cranberry mixture evenly over ham. Cover tightly with foil. Roast 1 hour. Spread $1/3$ cup more cranberry mixture over ham. Roast, covered, an additional 30 minutes to 1 hour or until internal temperature reaches 148°F when tested with meat thermometer inserted into thickest part of ham, not touching bone.

3. Preheat broiler. Remove foil; turn ham serving side up. Spread remaining cranberry mixture over top of ham. Broil 1 to 2 minutes until mixture glazes ham. Transfer ham to warm serving platter; let stand 5 minutes before serving. *Makes 10 to 12 servings*

# Roast Turkey
# with Sausage and Cornbread Stuffing

Roast Turkey
>    **1 Butterball® turkey (8 to 10 pounds)**
>    **2 tablespoons Happy Farms® butter, melted**

Sausage and Cornbread Stuffing

>    **1 package (16 ounces) Premium Pride®**
>       **pork sausage**
>  **1½ cups chopped onions**
>    **1 cup chopped celery**
>    **2 teaspoons poultry seasoning**
>    **1 teaspoon Spice Club® minced garlic**
>    **½ teaspoon Spice Club® black pepper**
>    **3 boxes (6 ounces each) Chef's Cupboard® cornbread stuffing mix**
>    **2 to 2½ cups water**
>    **1 can (14½ ounces) Chef's Cupboard® chicken broth**

1. Thaw turkey according to package directions.

2. For stuffing, brown sausage in large skillet over medium heat, stirring to break up meat; drain fat. Add onions, celery, poultry seasoning, garlic and pepper. Cook and stir 5 minutes or until vegetables are tender. Add stuffing mix, 2 cups water and broth; toss well. Add additional ¹/₂ cup water, if needed.

3. To heat stuffing separately, place stuffing in 13×9-baking dish sprayed with Ariel® no stick cooking spray. Tightly cover with Kwik-N-Fresh® aluminum foil; refrigerate until baking time. Let stand at room temperature 30 minutes before baking.

4. Preheat oven to 325°F. Spray shallow roasting pan and rack with Ariel® no stick cooking spray. Remove giblets from turkey. Rinse turkey and cavity in cold water; pat dry with paper towels. Brush skin with butter. To cook stuffing in turkey, fill neck and body cavities loosely with stuffing mixture. (Do not pack stuffing.) Return legs to original tucked position.

5. Place turkey, breast side up, on rack in roasting pan. Insert ovenproof meat thermometer into thickest part of thigh not touching bone. Roast turkey, uncovered, 3 to 3¹/₂ hours, basting occasionally with pan drippings until temperature reaches 180°F. If turkey is browning too quickly, tent loosely with Kwik-N-Fresh® aluminum foil, being careful not to touch meat thermometer. (If turkey is stuffed, roast 3³/₄ to 4¹/₂ hours. Thermometer inserted in center of stuffing should register 160°F.)

6. Transfer turkey to serving platter. Tent with Kwik-N-Fresh® aluminum foil; let stand 20 minutes. Place reserved stuffing in oven; increase temperature to 375°F. Bake, covered, 20 to 25 minutes or until hot. Slice turkey; serve with stuffing.

*Makes 8 to 10 servings*

# Holiday Pork Crown Roast
## with Apple Pecan Stuffing and Gravy

### Pork Roast and Gravy

**1 pork crown roast (about 7 pounds)**
**2 tablespoons Spice Club® minced garlic in olive oil**
**1 tablespoon dried rosemary**
**½ teaspoon Spice Club® black pepper**
**2 tablespoons Grandma's Best® flour**
**1 can (14½ ounces) Chef's Cupboard® chicken broth**

### Apple Pecan Stuffing

**½ cup (1 stick) Happy Farms® butter**
**1 large onion, finely chopped (about 1 cup)**
**2 teaspoons Spice Club® minced garlic**
**½ to 1 teaspoon Spice Club® black pepper**
**2 Gala or tart apples, peeled and finely diced (about 3 cups)**
**1 can (14½ ounces) Chef's Cupboard® chicken broth**
**1¼ cups water**
**2 packages (6 ounces each) Chef's Cupboard® cornbread stuffing mix**
**1 cup Southern Grove® coarsely chopped pecan halves**

1. Thaw roast according to package directions.

2. For pork roast, preheat oven to 325°F. Spray roasting pan with Ariel® no stick cooking spray. Place roast, bone side up, in shallow roasting pan. Cover bone tips with strips of Kwik-N-Fresh® aluminum foil. Combine garlic, rosemary and pepper in small bowl. Rub mixture over entire surface of roast.

3. Place meat thermometer in middle of roast, not touching bones. Roast 2 hours. Remove foil; continue roasting 45 to 60 minutes more or until meat thermometer registers 155°F. Transfer to another pan; tent with foil. Let stand 15 to 20 minutes. Temperature will continue to rise to 160°F. Remove netting.

4. For gravy, place roasting pan over large burner. Stir flour into drippings and brown particles in pan. Whisk in chicken broth. Cook and stir over medium heat until mixture is smooth and bubbly. Stir in additional juices from standing roast. Strain gravy, if desired. Keep warm over low heat.

5. For stuffing, melt butter in large saucepan. Add onion, garlic and black pepper; cook 5 minutes or until onions are tender, stirring occasionally. Add apple; cook 5 minutes. Add broth and water; bring to a simmer. Remove from heat; stir in stuffing mix and pecans. Cover; let stand 5 minutes. Fluff with fork; keep warm.

6. Transfer roast to serving platter. Place small amount of Apple Pecan Stuffing in center of rib bones. Cover tips of bones with foil frills. Garnish as desired. Serve with remaining stuffing and gravy.                                     *Makes 8 to 12 servings*

Prepare Ahead: Stuffing may be prepared up to 1 day before serving. Coat 1½-quart baking dish with Ariel® no stick cooking spray. Spoon stuffing into dish. Cover tightly with Kwik-N-Fresh® aluminum foil and store in the refrigerator. Let stand at room temperature 30 minutes before heating. Add a small amount of broth or water if needed for additional moisture. Bake in 350°F oven for 20 to 25 minutes or until heated through.

# Appleton® Baked Holiday Ham
# with Cranberry-Wine Compote

**2 teaspoons Carlini® vegetable oil**
**⅔ cup chopped onion**
**½ cup chopped celery**
**1 cup Burlwood® cabernet sauvignon wine**
**1 cup Golden Nectar® honey**
**½ cup Sweet Harvest® granulated sugar**
**1 package (12 ounces) fresh cranberries**
**1 Appleton® spiral sliced smoked honey ham half (about 7 to 8 pounds)**

1. For compote, heat oil in large saucepan over medium-high heat; add onion and celery. Cook and stir until tender. Stir in wine, honey and sugar; bring to a boil. Add cranberries; return to a boil. Reduce heat to low; cover and simmer 10 minutes. Cool completely.

2. Strain cranberry mixture; reserve 1 cup clear syrup. Transfer remaining syrup and cranberry mixture to small serving bowl; cover and refrigerate. Bring to room temperature 30 minutes before serving.

3. Preheat oven to 325°F. Line shallow roasting pan with Kwik-N-Fresh® aluminum foil. Discard glaze packet or save for another use.

4. Place ham face down in prepared pan. Brush ⅓ cup cranberry syrup evenly over ham. Cover tightly with foil. Roast 1 hour; brush ⅓ cup more cranberry syrup over ham. Roast, covered, 30 minutes to 1 hour more or until internal temperature reaches 148°F when tested with meat thermometer inserted into thickest part of ham not touching bone.

5. Turn on broiler. Remove foil. Turn ham serving side up. Spread remaining cranberry syrup over top of ham. Broil 1 to 2 minutes until syrup glazes ham. Transfer to warm serving platter; let stand 5 minutes before serving. Serve ham with Cranberry-Wine Compote. *Makes 10 to 12 servings*

### Wine Tip

*Burlwood® cabernet sauvignon is a medium to full-bodied wine with robust flavors of black cherry and blackberry touched with notes of toasted oak and spice. Enjoy with full-flavored meat or poultry dishes.*

# Kirkwood® Chicken Breasts
# with Festive Cranberry Sauce

### Chicken

**6 Kirkwood® boneless skinless chicken breasts**
**½ cup Grandma's Best® all-purpose flour**
**½ teaspoon Sebree® salt**
**½ teaspoon Spice Club® black pepper**
**¼ cup Carlini® canola oil**
**½ cup Chef's Cupboard® chicken broth**

### Festive Cranberry Sauce

**2 tablespoons Happy Farms® butter**
**1 small onion, finely chopped**
**1 teaspoon Spice Club® minced garlic**
**¼ teaspoon Sebree® salt**
**¼ teaspoon Spice Club® black pepper**
**1 can (15 ounces) Sweet Harvest® jellied cranberry sauce**
**½ cup Fit & Active® dried cranberries**
**½ cup Chef's Cupboard® chicken broth**
**2 tablespoons balsamic vinegar**

1. Thaw chicken breasts according to package directions.

2. For chicken, combine flour, salt and pepper in Kwik-N-Fresh® gallon food storage bag. Add chicken to bag; shake to coat completely with flour mixture.

3. Heat oil in large skillet over medium-high heat. Add chicken; cook in 2 batches until chicken is browned on both sides. Add chicken broth; bring to a boil. Reduce heat to low. Cover; simmer 10 to 15 minutes.

4. For sauce, melt butter in another large skillet over medium heat. Add onion, garlic, salt and pepper; cook and stir 5 minutes or until onion is softened. Stir in cranberry sauce, cranberries, chicken broth and vinegar. Reduce heat to medium. Cook and stir about 5 minutes or until cranberry sauce melts and mixture is heated through. Arrange chicken on platter. Drizzle sauce over chicken.                    *Makes 6 servings*

# Kirkwood® Stuffed Glazed Roast Chicken

### Chicken

**1 Kirkwood® whole chicken (4 to 5 pounds)**
**1 teaspoon Sebree® salt**
**½ teaspoon Spice Club® black pepper**
**2 tablespoons Carlini® vegetable oil**

### Stuffing

**¼ cup (½ stick) Happy Farms® butter**
**1 large apple, finely chopped**
**¼ cup thinly sliced celery**
**¼ cup chopped Southern Grove® walnuts**
**1 package (6 ounces) Chef's Cupboard® chicken flavor stuffing mix**
**¼ cup Sweet Harvest® raisins**
**½ teaspoon grated lemon peel**
**1½ cups water**

### Glaze

**½ cup Grandessa® peach & passion fruit spread**
**1 tablespoon Nature's Nectar® lemon juice**
**½ teaspoon ground cinnamon**

1. For chicken, thaw according to package directions.

2. For stuffing, melt butter in large saucepan over medium heat. Add apple and celery. Cook and stir 2 minutes. Add nuts. Cook 2 more minutes. Remove from heat. Add stuffing mix, raisins and lemon peel. Stir in water; mix well.

3. Preheat oven to 350°F. Sprinkle inside of chicken with salt and pepper; rub outside with oil. Just before roasting chicken, loosely fill body cavity with stuffing, if desired. Do not pack. Place chicken in shallow roasting pan. Cover loosely with Kwik-N-Fresh® aluminum foil; roast chicken 1 hour.

4. Place remaining stuffing in casserole sprayed with Ariel® no stick cooking spray. Tightly cover with Kwik-N-Fresh® aluminum foil. Place covered casserole in oven last 30 minutes of roasting time. Bake, covered, 25 to 30 minutes or until hot

5. For glaze, combine fruit spread, lemon juice and cinnamon in small saucepan. Cook and stir over low heat 3 minutes or until fruit spread melts and mixture is well blended.

6. Remove foil from chicken; brush with small amount of glaze. Roast chicken, uncovered, brushing frequently with glaze, 30 minutes more or until internal temperature reaches 180°F when tested with meat thermometer inserted into thickest part of thigh, not touching bone. Stuffing should reach 160°F when tested with an instant-read thermometer in center of stuffing. Let chicken stand 15 minutes before carving. Serve with stuffing.　　　　　　　　　　　　　　　　*Makes 4 servings*

# New York Strip Steaks
# with Mushroom Wine Sauce

## Mushroom Wine Sauce

**1 cup water**
**½ cup Winking Owl cabernet sauvignon wine**
**1 package (0.87 ounce) Spice Club brown gravy mix**
**¼ cup (½ stick) Happy Farms® butter**
**8 ounces sliced button mushrooms**
**6 to 8 ounces assorted wild mushrooms, sliced**
**¼ teaspoon dried thyme**

## Steaks

**4 Granger® New York strip steaks or T-bone steaks, thawed**
**Sebree® salt**
**Spice Club® black pepper**
**2 teaspoons minced parsley**

1. For sauce, combine water, wine and gravy mix in small bowl; mix well. Set aside.

2. Melt butter in large skillet over medium heat. Add mushrooms and thyme; cook and stir 5 minutes or until mushrooms release liquid. Cook 5 to 10 minutes more, stirring occasionally, until mushrooms turn brown and all liquid is evaporated.

3. Stir in gravy mixture. Simmer, uncovered, 5 to 10 minutes or until sauce is slightly thickened. Keep warm.

4. For steaks, broil or grill steaks 5 to 6 minutes per side or until desired doneness. Season with salt and pepper to taste. Serve with mushroom sauce. Sprinkle with parsley.

*Makes 4 servings*

### Wine Tip

*Winking Owl cabernet sauvignon is a medium bodied wine from* **ALDI**®*. You'll taste blackberry and plum complemented by the elegant aromas of vanilla and toasted oak. Winking Owl is a perfect wine for cooking and a wise choice with grilled meats.*

# Roast Turkey with Cranberry Stuffing

Roast Turkey
    **1 Butterball® turkey (8 to 10 pounds)**
    **2 tablespoons Carlini® extra virgin olive oil**

Cranberry Stuffing
    **1 cup coarsely chopped fresh cranberries**
    **2 tablespoons Sweet Harvest® sugar**
    **½ cup (1 stick) Happy Farms® butter**
    **1½ cups chopped onions**
    **1½ cups chopped celery**
    **2 teaspoons poultry seasoning**
    **½ teaspoon dried thyme**
    **½ teaspoon dried rosemary**
    **½ teaspoon Spice Club® black pepper**
    **3 boxes (6 ounces each) Chef's Cupboard® chicken or turkey flavor**
      **stuffing mix**
    **2 to 2½ cups water**
    **1 can (14½ ounces) Chef's Cupboard® chicken broth**

1. Thaw turkey according to package directions.

2. For turkey, preheat oven to 325°F. Spray shallow roasting pan and rack with Ariel® no stick cooking spray. Remove giblets from turkey. Rinse turkey and cavity in cold water; pat dry with paper towels. Brush skin with oil.

3. Place turkey, breast side up, on rack in roasting pan. Insert ovenproof meat thermometer into thickest part of thigh not touching bone. Roast turkey, uncovered, 3 to 3½ hours, basting occasionally with pan drippings until temperature reaches 180°F. If turkey is browning too quickly, tent loosely with Kwik-N-Fresh® aluminum foil, being careful not to touch meat thermometer.

4. For stuffing, combine cranberries and sugar in small bowl; set aside. Melt butter in large saucepan over medium heat. Add onions and celery. Cook and stir 8 minutes or until vegetables are tender; remove from heat. Stir in poultry seasoning, thyme, rosemary and pepper. Add stuffing mix and cranberry mixture; mix well. Drizzle 2 cups water and broth evenly over mixture; toss well. Add additional ¹/₂ cup water, if needed. Place stuffing in casserole sprayed with Ariel® no stick cooking spray. Tightly cover with Kwik-N-Fresh® aluminum foil; refrigerate until baking time. Let stand at room temperature 30 minutes before baking.

5. Transfer turkey to serving platter. Tent with Kwik-N-Fresh® aluminum foil; let stand 20 minutes. Place covered casserole of stuffing in oven; increase temperature to 375°F. Bake, covered, 20 to 25 minutes or until hot. Slice turkey; serve with stuffing.

*Makes 8 to 10 servings*

# Lush and Lovely Lodge Wreath

## supplies

- 20-inch artificial evergreen wreath of mixed greens

- 2 black chenille stems

- 1½ yards red and black plaid ribbon, 2½ inches wide

- Hot glue gun and glue sticks

- 10 pinecones

- 6 dried pomegranates

- Heavy-duty scissors or wire cutters

- Assorted foliage

- Berry clusters: 4 burgundy, 4 red

- 2 red berry sprays, 12 inches

1. Shape wreath to increase fullness and achieve a natural look. To make hanger, twist a chenille stem into loop on top back of wreath.

2. About 12 inches from one end of ribbon, form two 6-inch loops. Pinch loops together, and secure with chenille stem to form bow.

3. Glue bow to upper left side of wreath. Weave bow's streamers into wreath. Glue in place. Glue pinecones in wreath as shown.

4. Cut pomegranate stems to 1 inch. Glue 2 pomegranates in center of bow. Glue remaining pomegranates in clusters of 2, equally spaced around wreath.

5. Cut foliage into short lengths. Glue between pinecones and pomegranates. Glue a few sprigs over top of bow.

6. Glue burgundy berry clusters equally spaced around wreath; repeat with red berry clusters. Cut red berry sprays into 4-inch lengths. Glue into wreath as desired.

# Appleton® Pork Loin Roasts
## with Gingered Fruit Sauce

Pork Roasts
**2 Appleton® garlic & herb pork loin roasts (1½ to 2 pounds each)**

Gingered Fruit Sauce
**1 cup Wyalla Cove® or Burlwood® chardonnay wine**
**1 cup Nature's Nectar® cranberry apple juice**
**½ cup chopped Fit & Active® dried apricots**
**½ cup Fit & Active® dried cranberries**
**½ cup Grandessa® peach & passion fruit spread**
**¼ cup Sweet Harvest® premium golden raisins**
**½ teaspoon ground ginger**

1. For roasts, preheat oven to 350°F. Tie roasts with string, if desired.

2. Place roasts on broiler pan or on rack in large roasting pan. Roast 45 to 60 minutes or until internal temperature reaches 155°F when tested with meat thermometer inserted into thickest part of roasts. Transfer roasts to cutting board; tent with Kwik-N-Fresh® foil. Let stand 10 minutes. (Internal temperature will continue to rise 5° to 10°F during stand time.)

3. For sauce, combine wine, cranberry apple juice, apricots, cranberries, fruit spread, raisins and ginger in large saucepan. Bring to a boil over medium-high heat. Boil 10 to 15 minutes or until slightly thickened, stirring frequently.

4. Carve pork into thin slices. Serve with sauce.　　　　　　　*Makes 6 to 8 servings*

# Sea Queen® Salmon
# with Cranberry-Poblano Salsa

**4 Sea Queen® salmon fillets**
**⅔ cup Happy Harvest® crushed pineapple in juice**
**1 poblano chile pepper, finely chopped**
**½ cup Fit & Active® dried cranberries**
**¼ cup finely chopped red onion**
**2 tablespoons Nature's Nectar® lemon juice**
**1 to 2 tablespoons chopped fresh cilantro or parsley**
**1 tablespoon pineapple juice**
**1 teaspoon grated lemon peel**
**1 teaspoon Spice Club® seasoned salt**
**½ teaspoon Spice Club® black pepper**

1. Thaw salmon in refrigerator according to package directions.

2. For salsa, combine pineapple, poblano, cranberries, onion, lemon juice, cilantro, pineapple juice and lemon peel, if desired. Toss gently until thoroughly blended; set aside.

3. Preheat broiler. Spray broiler pan and rack with Ariel® no stick cooking spray.

4. Arrange salmon on rack. Sprinkle ½ teaspoon seasoned salt and ¼ teaspoon pepper evenly over salmon. Broil 3 minutes. Turn; sprinkle remaining seasoned salt and pepper over salmon. Broil 3 minutes more or until almost opaque in center. Serve salmon with salsa.

*Makes 4 to 6 servings*

**ALDI**

# Appleton® Pork Loin Roasts
# with Cherry Sauce

### Pork Roasts
**2 Appleton® garlic & herb pork loin roasts (1½ to 2 pounds each)**

### Cherry Sauce
**1 jar (8.8 ounces) Grandessa® morello cherry fruit spread**
**¼ cup Chef's Cupboard® chicken broth**
**2 tablespoons Burlwood® cabernet sauvignon wine**
**1 teaspoon Spice Club® minced garlic in olive oil**
**1 teaspoon Briargate® Dijon mustard**
**1 teaspoon grated orange peel**

1. Preheat oven to 350°F.

2. For roasts, place 6 inches apart on broiler pan or on rack in large shallow roasting pan. Roast 45 to 60 minutes or until internal temperature reaches 155°F when tested with meat thermometer inserted into thickest part of roasts. Transfer roasts to cutting board; tent with Kwik-N-Fresh® foil. Let stand 10 minutes. (Internal temperature will continue to rise 5° to 10°F during stand time.)

3. For sauce, combine fruit spread, broth, wine, garlic, mustard and orange peel in medium saucepan. Bring to a boil over medium-high heat. Cook 5 to 10 minutes or until sauce is slightly thickened.

4. Carve pork into thin slices; place on serving platter. Pour ½ cup cherry sauce around pork. Serve with remaining sauce.                        *Makes 6 to 8 servings*

# Maple-Glazed Ham
# and Whipped Sweet Potatoes

**¼ cup Aunt Maple's® pancake syrup**
**1 teaspoon Briargate® Dijon mustard**
**2 Appleton® ham center slices (about 1 pound each)**
**Whipped Sweet Potatoes (recipe follows)**

Combine syrup and mustard in small bowl; set aside. Heat large skillet over medium heat. Place ham in skillet; brush with glaze. Cook 3 minutes on each side; turning and basting with glaze until hot. Cut each steak in half to serve. Serve with Whipped Sweet Potatoes.

*Makes 4 servings*

## Whipped Sweet Potatoes

**1 can (15 ounces) Happy Harvest® cut sweet potatoes, drained**
**2 tablespoons Aunt Maple's® pancake syrup**
**2 tablespoons Happy Farms® butter**
**½ teaspoon Sebree® salt**
**¼ teaspoon Spice Club® black pepper**

Place potatoes in medium microwavable bowl. Add syrup, butter, salt and pepper. Beat with electric mixer on medium speed until light and fluffy. Microwave on HIGH 3 to 5 minutes or until hot.

*Makes 4 servings*

## HOLIDAY TIP

*Put a delicious dinner on the table in under 30 minutes. Serve this ham and sweet potato recipe with Happy Harvest® green beans and a tossed salad made with Freshire Farms® salad mix, your favorite SaladMate® Fit & Active® salad dressing, a diced apple and Southern Grove® walnuts.*

# Granger® Strip Steaks
# with Mushrooms and Couscous

**1 can (14½ ounces) Chef's Cupboard® beef broth, divided**
**1 cup Happy Harvest® frozen green peas**
**½ teaspoon Spice Club® black pepper, divided**
**1 cup uncooked couscous**
**3 tablespoons Happy Farms® butter, divided**
**4 Granger® New York strip steaks, thawed**
**8 ounces sliced button or wild mushrooms, such as portobello or shiitake**
**¼ cup finely chopped onion or chopped green onions**
**1 teaspoon Briargate® Dijon mustard**
**1 teaspoon Worcestershire sauce**

1. Reserve ¼ cup broth. Bring remaining broth, peas and ¼ teaspoon pepper to a boil in medium saucepan over high heat. Stir in couscous; cover and remove from heat. Let stand while preparing steaks.

2. Melt 1 tablespoon butter in large skillet over medium-high heat. Sprinkle both sides of steaks with pepper; add 2 steaks to skillet. Cook 3 to 4 minutes per side for medium-rare or to desired doneness. Transfer to plate; keep warm. Repeat with remaining 2 steaks and 1 tablespoon butter. Transfer to platter; cover and keep warm.

3. Melt remaining 1 tablespoon butter in same skillet; add mushrooms and onion. Cook 2 minutes, stirring occasionally. Stir in reserved ¼ cup broth, mustard and Worcestershire sauce. Simmer 2 minutes. Return steaks to skillet; heat through, turning steaks and stirring mushrooms once.

4. Spoon couscous mixture evenly onto 4 serving plates. Top each with 1 steak and mushrooms.

*Makes 4 servings*

# CHAPTER 4

# Dazzling Desserts

## Gingered Pumpkin Custard

¾ cup Sweet Harvest® granulated sugar
2 Goldhen® eggs
1½ teaspoons ground cinnamon
½ teaspoon Sebree® salt
½ teaspoon nutmeg
1 can (15 ounces) Sweet Harvest® solid pack pumpkin
1¼ cups Friendly Farms half & half
3 tablespoons chopped candied ginger
 Friendly Farms aerosol whipped cream
 Colored sprinkles (optional)

1. Preheat oven to 375°F. Grease 6 or 8 custard cups or ramekins with Happy Farms® butter.

2. Combine sugar, eggs, cinnamon, salt and nutmeg in medium bowl; mix well. Add pumpkin and half & half. Mix until well blended. Pour into prepared cups. Sprinkle ginger evenly over top of pumpkin mixture. Place cups on baking sheet.

3. Bake 35 to 40 minutes or until knife inserted into centers comes out clean. Cool on wire rack at least 20 minutes before serving. Serve warm or at room temperature. Garnish with whipped cream and sprinkles. *Makes 6 to 8 servings*

Variation: Pour custard mixture into greased 1½-quart casserole or 8-inch glass baking dish. Bake 45 minutes or until knife inserted into center comes out clean.

# Chocolate Marble and Praline Cheesecake

Crust
   **1½ cups crushed Mercer® vanilla wafers**
   **½ cup finely chopped toasted Southern Grove® pecans***
   **¼ cup Sweet Harvest® powdered sugar**
   **¼ cup (½ stick) Happy Farms® butter, melted**

Filling
   **1 cup Sweet Harvest® packed light brown sugar**
   **2 tablespoons Grandma's Best® all-purpose flour**
   **3 packages (8 ounces each) Happy Farms® cream cheese, softened**
   **3 Goldhen® eggs, lightly beaten**
   **1½ teaspoons Spice Club vanilla**
   **½ cup Baker's Corner® real semi sweet chocolate chips, melted**
   **20 to 25 Southern Grove® pecan halves (½ cup)**
      **Caramel ice cream topping**

*To toast pecans, place whole nuts on baking sheet. Bake at 350°F 5 to 7 minutes or until lightly browned, stirring frequently. Or, spread in single layer on plate. Microwave 1 to 2 minutes, stirring every 30 seconds.*

1. Preheat oven to 350°F.

2. For crust, combine wafer crumbs, pecans, powdered sugar and butter in large bowl; mix well. Press mixture onto bottom and up side of ungreased 9-inch springform pan. Bake 10 to 15 minutes or until lightly browned. Transfer to wire rack.

3. For filling, combine brown sugar and flour in small bowl; mix well. Beat cream cheese in large bowl with electric mixer at low speed until fluffy; gradually add brown sugar mixture. Add eggs and vanilla; beat just until blended. Remove 1 cup batter to small bowl; stir in chocolate. Pour remaining plain batter over warm crust.

4. Drop spoonfuls of chocolate batter over plain batter. Run knife through batters to marbleize. Arrange pecan halves around edge. Bake 45 to 55 minutes or until set. Loosen cake from side of pan. Cool completely on wire rack. Refrigerate 2 hours or until ready to serve.

5. To serve, remove side of pan. Spread caramel topping over top of cheesecake.

*Makes 12 to 16 servings*

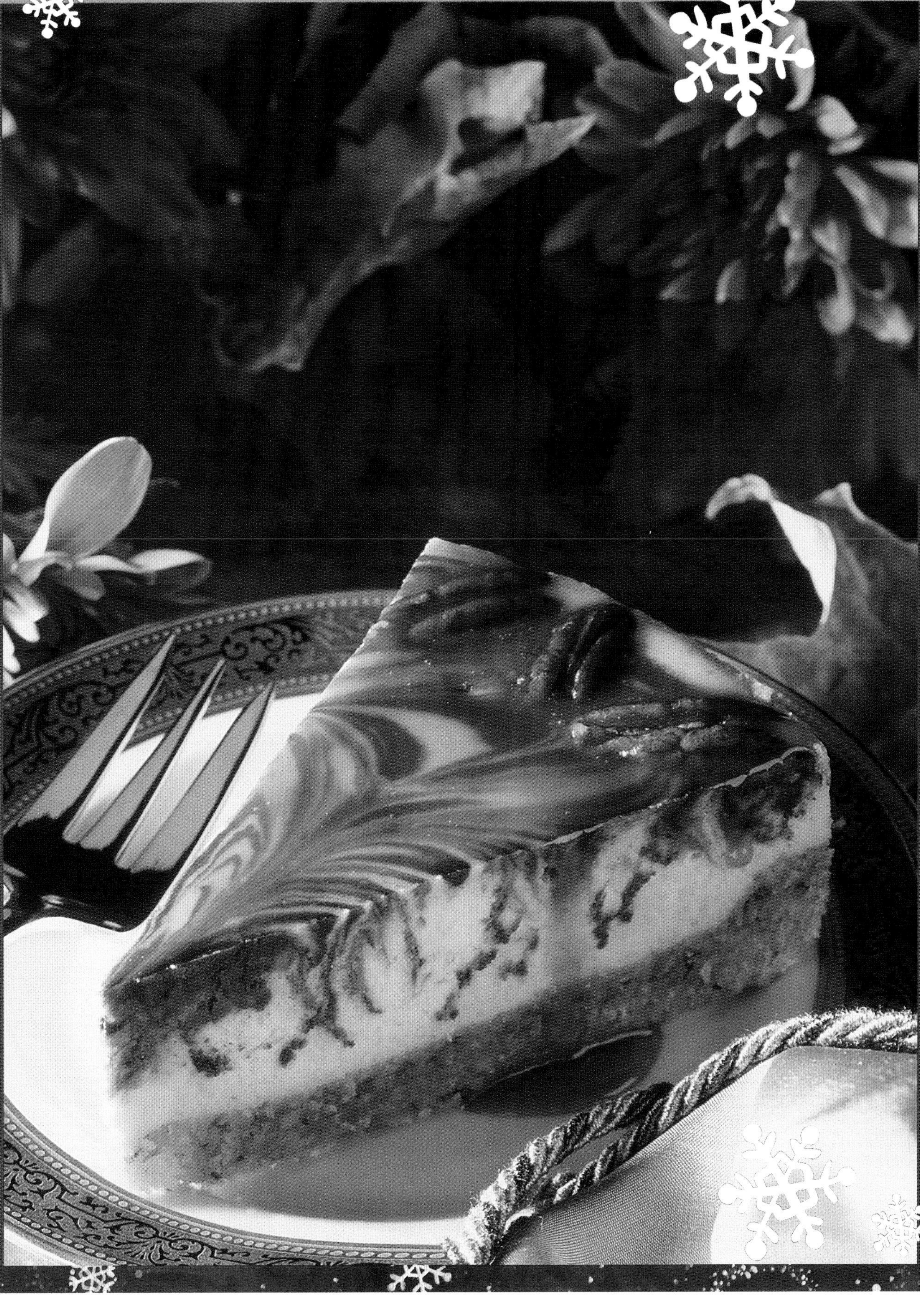

# Cranberry-Lime Chiffon Pie

**40 to 50 Clancy's® mini twist pretzels (about ¼ bag)**
**½ cup (1 stick) Happy Farms® butter, melted**
**¼ cup Sweet Harvest® granulated sugar**
**1 can (16 ounces) Sweet Harvest® jellied cranberry sauce**
**2½ teaspoons grated lime peel (2 limes)**
**1 jar (7 ounces) Baker's Corner® marshmallow crème**
**3 cups Sundae Shoppe® frozen whipped topping, thawed**

1. Grease 9-inch pie pan with Carlini® vegetable shortening. Crush pretzels in Kwik-N-Fresh® gallon plastic food storage bag with rolling pin to measure 1⅓ cups. Combine pretzel crumbs, butter and sugar in medium bowl until well blended. Press onto bottom and up side of prepared pan.

2. Combine cranberry sauce and lime peel in large bowl; mix well. Reserve ⅓ cup mixture. Add marshmallow crème to remaining cranberry mixture; mix well. Gently fold in whipped topping. Spoon mixture evenly into prepared crust. Freeze at least 4 hours or up to 3 days. Cover with Kwik-N-Fresh® aluminum foil after 2 hours.

3. To serve, spoon reserved ⅓ cup cranberry mixture in ring around center of pie.

*Makes 1 (9-inch) pie*

# Chocolate Cream-Filled Cake Roll

¾ cup sifted Grandma's Best® all-purpose flour
¼ cup Baker's Corner baking cocoa
½ teaspoon Baker's Corner® baking powder
¼ teaspoon Sebree® salt
4 Goldhen® eggs
¾ cup Sweet Harvest® granulated sugar
1 tablespoon water
1 teaspoon Spice Club vanilla
  Sweet Harvest® powdered sugar
  Cream Filling (page 73)
  Chocolate Stars (page 73)
1 can Friendly Farms aerosol whipped cream
  Fresh raspberries and mint leaves (optional)

1. Preheat oven to 375°F. Grease bottom of 15½×10½×1-inch jelly-roll pan. Line with waxed paper. Grease paper and sides of pan; dust with flour. Combine flour, cocoa, baking powder and salt in small bowl; set aside.

2. Beat eggs in large bowl with electric mixer at high speed about 5 minutes or until thick and lemon colored. Add granulated sugar, a little at a time, beating at medium speed until thick and fluffy. Beat in water and vanilla. Fold in flour mixture at low speed until smooth. Spread evenly in prepared pan.

3. Bake 12 to 15 minutes or until toothpick inserted into center comes out clean. Meanwhile, sprinkle clean towel with powdered sugar. Loosen cake edges; invert onto prepared towel. Carefully peel off waxed paper. Roll up cake with towel inside, starting with narrow end. Cool, seam side down, 20 minutes on wire rack.

4. Meanwhile, prepare Cream Filling and Chocolate Stars. Unroll cake and spread with Cream Filling. Roll up again, without towel. Cover; refrigerate at least 1 hour before serving. Dust with additional powdered sugar before serving. Make rosettes with whipped cream on top of cake. Place points of Chocolate Stars in rosettes. Garnish with raspberries and mint. Store tightly covered in refrigerator.   *Makes 8 to 10 servings*

# Cream Filling

**1 teaspoon unflavored gelatin**
**¼ cup cold water**
**1 cup Friendly Farms whipping cream**
**2 tablespoons Sweet Harvest® powdered sugar**
**1 tablespoon orange-flavored liqueur**

Sprinkle gelatin over cold water in small saucepan; let stand 1 minute to soften. Heat over low heat until dissolved, stirring constantly. Cool to room temperature. Beat cream, powdered sugar and liqueur in small chilled bowl with electric mixer at high speed until stiff peaks form. Beat in gelatin mixture at low speed. Cover; refrigerate 5 to 10 minutes.

Chocolate Stars: Melt 1 cup Baker's Corner® real semi sweet chocolate chips in small saucepan over low heat, stirring frequently. Pour onto waxed-paper-lined cookie sheet. Spread to ⅛-inch thickness with small metal spatula. Refrigerate about 15 minutes or until firm. Cut out stars with cookie cutter. Carefully lift stars from waxed paper using metal spatula or knife. Refrigerate until ready to use.

# Cran-Raspberry Trifle

**1 package (3.5 ounces) Mr. Pudding® instant vanilla pudding**
**½ teaspoon almond extract**
**1 package (about 11 ounces) frozen pound cake, thawed**
**1 can (21 ounces) raspberry pie filling**
**1 can (16 ounces) Sweet Harvest® jellied cranberry sauce**
**Sundae Shoppe® frozen whipped topping, fresh raspberries**
**and fresh mint sprigs**

1. Prepare pudding according to package directions. Cut pound cake into ³/₄-inch cubes. Combine raspberry pie filling and cranberry sauce in medium bowl; blend well.

2. Layer one third of cake cubes, one third of raspberry mixture and one third of prepared pudding in 1¹/₂- to 2-quart straight-sided glass serving bowl. Repeat layers twice. Cover; refrigerate until serving time. Garnish with whipped topping, raspberries and mint sprigs.

*Makes 8 servings*

## Elegant Wire Ornaments

### supplies

- 36-inch length 18-gauge steel spool wire
- Needle-nose pliers
- Wire cutters
- 2 beads
- 14 inches silver cord

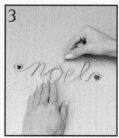

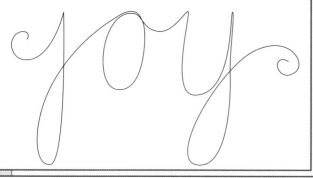

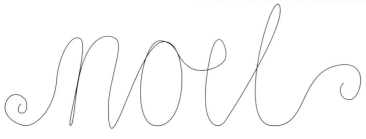

1. Use needle-nose pliers to bend wire into letter shapes, using one of the patterns for a guide. Trim excess wire with wire cutters.

2. Slip bead onto each end of wire. Use pliers to make small loop at end of the wire to prevent bead from slipping off.

3. Fold the cord in half, and knot the loose ends. Tie cord around the top of the letter O for hanger.

# Old-Fashioned Gingerbread

**2 cups Grandma's Best® all-purpose flour**
**2 teaspoons ground ginger**
**1 teaspoon Baker's Corner® baking soda**
**1 teaspoon ground cinnamon**
**½ teaspoon Sebree® salt**
**¼ teaspoon ground cloves**
**1 tablespoon Beaumont® instant coffee**
**¼ cup hot water**
**½ cup (1 stick) Happy Farms® butter, softened**
**½ cup Sweet Harvest® packed light brown sugar**
**1 cup molasses**
**1 Goldhen® egg**
**¾ cup buttermilk**
**Sundae Shoppe® frozen whipped topping, thawed**

1. Preheat oven to 350°F. Spray 9-inch square or 11×7-inch baking pan with Ariel® no stick cooking spray; set aside. Combine flour, ginger, baking soda, cinnamon, salt and cloves in medium bowl; set aside. Dissolve coffee granules in hot water; cool.

2. Combine butter and sugar in large bowl. Beat with electric mixer at medium speed until fluffy. Add molasses and egg; beat well. Add coffee; blend well. Alternately add flour mixture and buttermilk; beat just until mixed.

3. Pour batter into prepared pan. Bake 40 to 45 minutes or until toothpick inserted into center comes out clean. Cool in pan on wire rack. Serve with whipped topping.

*Makes 8 to 12 servings*

Variation: For an alternate topping, dust top of cake lightly with Sweet Harvest® powdered sugar. For a decorative appearance, place doily on top of cake before dusting. Carefully lift doily from cake.

# The Best Pumpkin Pie

**1 can (15 ounces) Sweet Harvest® solid pack pumpkin**
**¾ cup Sweet Harvest® packed light brown sugar**
**2 teaspoons ground cinnamon**
**1½ teaspoons ground ginger**
**½ teaspoon ground nutmeg**
**½ teaspoon Sebree® salt**
**¼ teaspoon ground cloves**
**4 Goldhen® eggs, lightly beaten**
**1½ cups Friendly Farms half & half**
**1 teaspoon Spice Club vanilla**
**1 Buehler's® refrigerated pie crust**
**1 can Friendly Farms aerosol whipped cream**

1. Preheat oven to 400°F.

2. Combine pumpkin and brown sugar in large bowl; mix well. Stir in cinnamon, ginger, nutmeg, salt and cloves. Add eggs; mix well. Gradually stir in half & half and vanilla; mix until combined. Pour pumpkin mixture into unbaked pie crust. Place on cookie sheet. Bake any extra filling in greased small ovenproof custard cup.

3. Bake 15 minutes. Reduce heat to 350°F. Bake 40 to 45 minutes or until knife inserted near center comes out clean. Cool on wire rack. Serve with whipped cream.

*Makes 1 (9-inch) pie*

# Fun and Fruity Upside-Down Cake

1¼ cups Grandma's Best® sifted all-purpose flour
2 teaspoons Baker's Corner® baking powder
¼ teaspoon Sebree® salt
1¼ cups Sweet Harvest® packed light brown sugar, divided
½ cup (1 stick) Happy Farms® butter, softened, divided
1 Goldhen® egg
½ cup Friendly Farms® milk
½ teaspoon Spice Club vanilla
½ teaspoon grated lemon peel or lemon extract
1 can (20 ounces) Sweet Harvest® crushed pineapple, well drained
1 jar (10 ounces) Sweet Harvest® maraschino cherries, drained

1. Preheat oven to 350°F. Combine flour, baking powder and salt in medium bowl; set aside.

2. Beat ³/₄ cup brown sugar and ¹/₄ cup butter in large bowl with electric mixer at medium speed until light and fluffy. Beat in egg. Add flour mixture alternately with milk, beating well at low speed after each addition. Blend in vanilla and lemon peel.

3. Melt remaining ¹/₄ cup butter in 9-inch cake pan or 9-inch ovenproof skillet. Stir in remaining ¹/₂ cup brown sugar. Spread sugar mixture to evenly cover bottom of pan. Top brown sugar mixture with pineapple.

4. Reserve several whole cherries for garnish. Cut remaining cherries in half; spoon over pineapple. Pour batter over fruit. Bake 40 to 50 minutes or until toothpick inserted into center comes out clean.

5. Cool cake in pan on wire rack 10 minutes. Loosen edges; turn upside down onto cake plate. Garnish with reserved cherries. *Makes 1 (9-inch) cake*

## HOLIDAY TIP

*Stock up on a variety of decorative and delicious toppings for desserts such as Friendly Farms aerosol whipped cream and Sundae Shoppe® ice creams and whipped topping. Make chocolate curls with Choceur® chocolate bars to sprinkle over the toppings.*

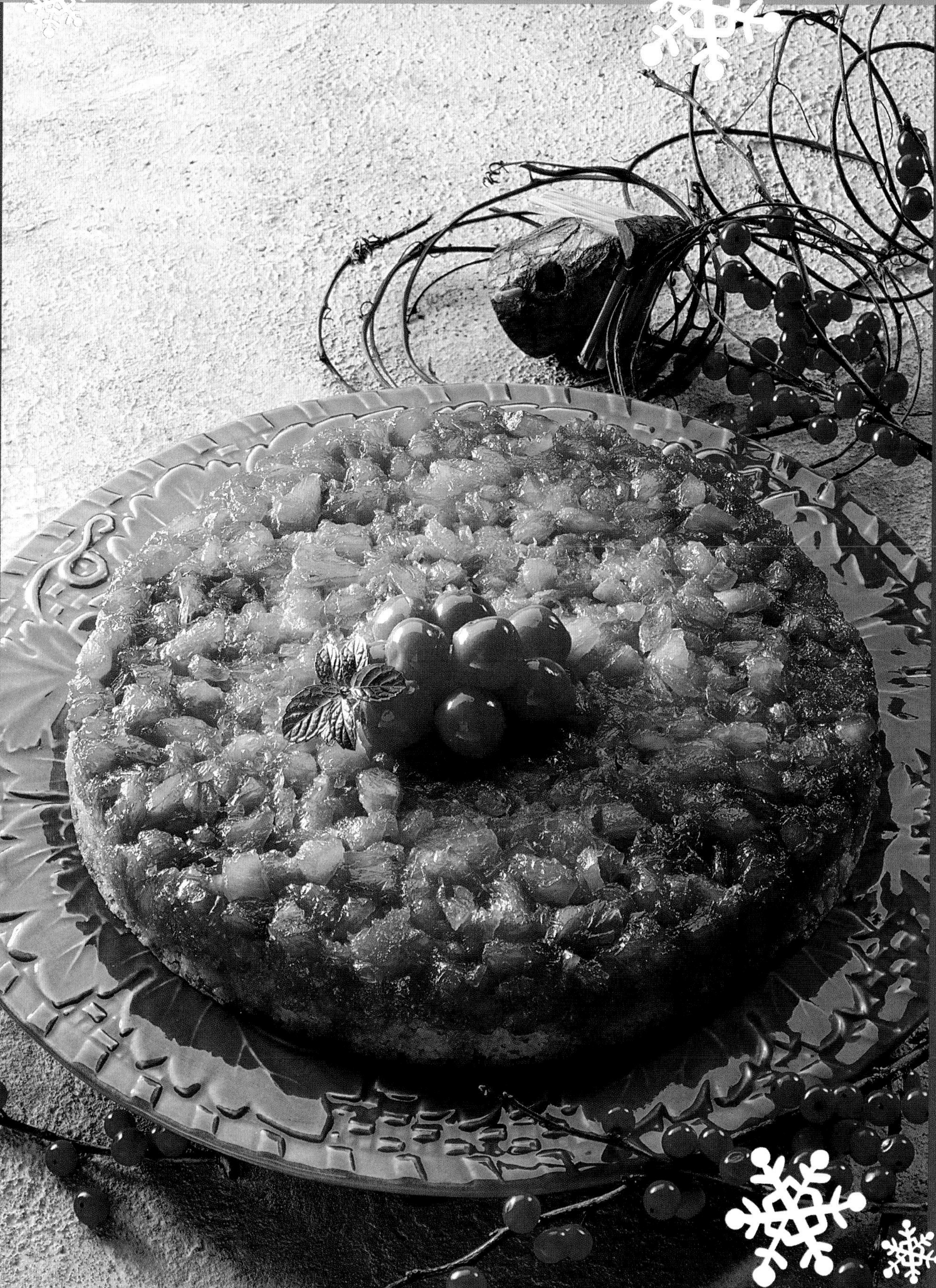

# CHAPTER 5

# Yuletide Treats

## Candy Cane Fudge

½ cup **Friendly Farms whipping cream**
½ cup **Baker's Corner light corn syrup**
3 cups **Baker's Corner® real semi sweet chocolate chips**
1½ cups **Sweet Harvest® powdered sugar, sifted**
1 cup **crushed Mystik® starlite mints**
1½ teaspoons **Spice Club vanilla**

1. Line 8-inch baking pan with Kwik-N-Fresh® aluminum foil, extending edges over sides of pan.

2. Bring cream and corn syrup to a boil in 2-quart saucepan over medium heat. Boil 1 minute. Remove from heat. Add chocolate chips; stir constantly until chips are melted. Stir in powdered sugar, mints and vanilla. Pour into prepared pan. Spread mixture into corners. Cover; refrigerate 2 hours or until firm.

3. Lift fudge out of pan using foil; remove foil. Cut into 1-inch squares. Store in airtight container. *Makes about 2 pounds (64 pieces)*

# Ginger Shortbread Delights

**1 cup (2 sticks) Happy Farms® butter, softened**
**½ cup Sweet Harvest® powdered sugar**
**⅓ cup Sweet Harvest® packed light brown sugar**
**½ teaspoon Sebree® salt**
**2 cups minus 2 tablespoons Grandma's Best® all-purpose flour**
**4 ounces crystallized ginger**

## Chocolate Glaze
**⅓ bar (11 rectangles) Choceur® milk chocolate, broken into small pieces**
**2 tablespoons Happy Farms® butter**
**2 tablespoons Friendly Farms whipping cream**
**1 tablespoon Sweet Harvest® powdered sugar**
**⅛ teaspoon Sebree® salt**

1. Preheat oven to 300°F.

2. Beat butter, sugars and salt in large bowl with electric mixer at medium speed until creamy. Gradually add flour; beat until well blended.

3. Shape dough by tablespoons into balls. Place 1 inch apart on ungreased cookie sheets; flatten to ¹/₂-inch thickness. Cut ginger into ¹/₄-inch-thick slices. Place 1 slice ginger on top of each cookie.

4. Bake 20 minutes or until set and lightly browned. Cool 5 minutes on cookie sheets. Remove to wire racks to cool completely.

5. For Chocolate Glaze, melt chocolate and butter in top of double boiler over simmering water. (Do not boil.) Remove from heat. Add cream, powdered sugar and salt; stir until smooth. Drizzle chocolate over cookies. Let stand about 30 minutes or until glaze is set.

*Makes about 3¹/₂ dozen cookies*

Variations: Use a variety of nuts instead of ginger for other fabulous cookies. Place a Southern Grove® pecan or walnut half in the center of each flattened ball. Or, roll balls in chopped nuts before flattening.

# Peppermint Patties

**2 cups Grandma's Best® all-purpose flour**
**½ cup plus 1 tablespoon Baker's Corner baking cocoa, sifted, divided**
**1 teaspoon Baker's Corner® baking powder**
**½ teaspoon Sebree® salt**
**1 cup Sweet Harvest® granulated sugar**
**¾ cup (1½ sticks) Happy Farms® butter, softened**
**1 Goldhen® egg**
**4 teaspoons Spice Club vanilla, divided**
**1½ teaspoons peppermint extract**
**3 cups Sweet Harvest® powdered sugar**
**¼ cup hot water or milk (not boiling)**

1. Combine flour, ½ cup cocoa, baking powder and salt in small bowl; set aside. Beat granulated sugar and butter in large bowl with electric mixer at medium speed 1 minute or until creamy. Add egg, 1 teaspoon vanilla and peppermint extract; beat until well blended. Gradually stir in flour mixture just until blended.

2. Shape dough into 12×2-inch log on lightly floured work surface. Wrap tightly in waxed paper, then wrap in Kwik-N-Fresh® plastic wrap. Freeze 2 hours or until firm.

3. Preheat oven to 350°F. Grease cookie sheets with Carlini® vegetable shortening. Cut dough into ⅛-inch slices. Place slices 1 inch apart on prepared cookie sheets. Bake 9 minutes or until puffed and firm to the touch. Cool on cookie sheets 1 to 2 minutes. Transfer to wire racks to cool completely.

4. For icing, combine powdered sugar, hot water and remaining 3 teaspoons vanilla in medium bowl; stir until smooth. Add additional water, ½ teaspoon at a time, if necessary, until desired consistency is reached. Divide icing in half. Add remaining 1 tablespoon cocoa powder to one bowl; stir until well blended. Cover cocoa icing; set aside.

5. Frost cooled cookies with vanilla icing; let stand until set. Drizzle cookies with chocolate icing; let stand until set.　　　　　　*Makes about 4 dozen cookies*

# Traditional Peanut Brittle

**1½ cups Fit & Active® unsalted peanuts**
**1 cup Sweet Harvest® granulated sugar**
**1 cup Baker's Corner light corn syrup**
**¼ cup water**
**2 tablespoons Happy Farms® butter**
**¼ teaspoon Baker's Corner® baking soda**

1. Heavily butter large cookie sheet; set aside. Place peanuts in ungreased 8-inch square baking pan. To warm peanuts, place in oven and heat oven to 250°F.

2. Meanwhile, place sugar, corn syrup, water and butter in heavy 2-quart saucepan. Stir over medium-low heat until sugar is dissolved and mixture comes to a boil, being careful not to splash sugar mixture on side of pan. Carefully clip candy thermometer to side of pan (do not let bulb touch bottom of pan). Cook over medium-low heat without stirring until thermometer registers 280°F. Gradually stir in warm peanuts. Cook until thermometer registers 300°F (hard-crack stage), stirring frequently.

3. Immediately remove from heat; stir in baking soda until thoroughly blended. (Mixture will froth and foam.) Immediately pour onto prepared cookie sheet. Spread mixture to form even layer. Cool about 30 minutes or until set. Break brittle into pieces. Store in airtight container.                                    *Makes about 1¹/₂ pounds*

# Jolly Jingle Bell Candleholder

## supplies

- 2×2 inches foam

- 9-inch-tall clear glass cylindrical vase with 3¼-inch opening

- Low-temperature glue gun and glue sticks

- 8 evergreen sprigs, 6 inches each

- Wire cutters

- Scissors

- 3 sheet music pages

- 1 yard gold metallic ribbon, 1¾ inches wide

- Ruler

- Floral wire

- 2 red berry sprays, 12 inches each

- 6 holly leaves

- 48 gold jingle bells, assorted sizes

- Clear glass votive holder

- Red votive candle

1. Glue foam block to bottom of vase. This is where you will insert evergreens.

2. Place vase so foam block is on your right side. Insert and glue 2 evergreen sprigs horizontally at base of foam, one coming in front of foam and one extending away from foam. Cut evergreens into short lengths. Fill in around already inserted evergreens.

3. Cut pages of sheet music in half horizontally. Tightly roll each section, and glue edges in place to secure. Cut 1 music roll in half. Insert and glue all rolled pages into evergreens.

4. About 6 inches from one end of gold ribbon, shape 2 loops about 3½ inches each. Pinch 2 loops together. Secure with short length of floral wire. Trim end of bow streamers to 4 inches. Cut V shape into end of each. Glue remaining ribbon trailing out back of design. Trim end of ribbon into V shape.

5. Cut 1 red berry spray in half. Insert a length vertically behind bow. Insert other section coming forward beneath bow. Cut other berry spray into short lengths and insert around bow. Glue holly leaves into design around bow and music. Glue jingle bell to middle of bow. Add more jingle bells as desired.

6. Fill vase with assorted jingle bells to about 3 inches from top. Place votive holder with candle inside vase.

# Chocolate Gingerbread Cookies

2¼ cups Grandma's Best® all-purpose flour
  3 tablespoons Baker's Corner baking cocoa
2½ teaspoons ground ginger
  ½ teaspoon Baker's Corner® baking soda
  ½ teaspoon ground cinnamon
  ⅛ teaspoon Sebree® salt
  ⅛ teaspoon Spice Club® black pepper
  ½ cup (1 stick) Happy Farms® butter, softened
  ½ cup Sweet Harvest® packed light brown sugar
  ¼ cup Sweet Harvest® granulated sugar
  1 tablespoon Carlini® vegetable shortening
  ¾ cup (4 ounces) Baker's Corner® real semi sweet chocolate chips,
     melted and cooled
  2 tablespoons molasses
  1 Goldhen® egg
    Baker's Corner® vanilla frosting

1. Combine flour, cocoa, ginger, baking soda, cinnamon, salt and pepper in medium bowl; set aside. Beat butter, sugars and shortening in large bowl with electric mixer at medium speed until creamy. Add chocolate; beat until blended. Add molasses and egg; beat until well blended. Gradually add flour mixture to butter mixture, beating until well blended. Divide dough in half. Wrap each half in Kwik-N-Fresh® plastic wrap; refrigerate at least 1 hour.

2. Preheat oven to 350°F. Roll out half of dough between sheets of Kwik-N-Fresh® plastic wrap to about ¹/₄-inch thickness. Cut out shapes with 5-inch cookie cutters; place cutouts on ungreased cookie sheets. Refrigerate at least 15 minutes. Repeat with remaining dough.

3. Bake 8 to 10 minutes or until cookies have puffed slightly and have small crackles on surfaces. Cool 5 minutes on cookie sheets; remove to wire racks to cool completely. Decorate cooled cookies with frosting.     *Makes about 2 dozen (5-inch) cookies*

Chewy Chocolate Gingerbread Drops: Decrease flour to 1³/₄ cups. Shape 1¹/₂ teaspoonfuls of dough into balls. Place on ungreased cookie sheets. Flatten balls slightly and do not refrigerate before baking. Bake as directed above.

# Chocolate Surprise Cookies

**2¾ cups Grandma's Best® all-purpose flour**
**¾ cup Baker's Corner baking cocoa**
**½ teaspoon Baker's Corner® baking powder**
**½ teaspoon Baker's Corner® baking soda**
**1 cup (2 sticks) Happy Farms® butter, softened**
**1½ cups Sweet Harvest® packed light brown sugar**
**½ cup plus 1 tablespoon Sweet Harvest® granulated sugar, divided**
**2 Goldhen® eggs**
**1 teaspoon Spice Club vanilla**
**1 cup Southern Grove® chopped pecans, divided**
**1 package (9 ounces) caramels coated in milk chocolate**
**½ package (about 3.5 ounces) Choceur® white chocolate, coarsely chopped**

1. Combine flour, cocoa, baking powder and baking soda in medium bowl; set aside.

2. Beat butter, brown sugar and ¹/₂ cup granulated sugar with electric mixer at medium speed until light and fluffy; beat in eggs and vanilla. Gradually add flour mixture and ¹/₂ cup pecans; beat well. Cover dough; refrigerate 15 minutes or until firm enough to roll into balls.

3. Preheat oven to 375°F. Place remaining ¹/₂ cup pecans and 1 tablespoon sugar in shallow dish. Roll tablespoonful of dough around 1 caramel candy, covering completely; press one side into nut mixture. Place, nut side up, on ungreased cookie sheet. Repeat with remaining dough and candies, placing 3 inches apart.

4. Bake 10 to 12 minutes or until set and slightly cracked. Let stand on cookie sheet 2 minutes. Transfer cookies to wire rack; cool completely.

5. Place white chocolate in Kwik-N-Fresh® plastic freezer bag; seal bag. Microwave on MEDIUM (50% power) 30 seconds. Knead bag to smooth chocolate. Microwave at additional 15 seconds intervals or just until chocolate is melted when kneaded. Cut off tiny corner of bag; drizzle chocolate onto cookies. Let stand about 30 minutes or until chocolate is set.                        *Makes about 3¹/₂ dozen cookies*

# Triple Layer Chocolate Mints

**1 cup (6 ounces) Baker's Corner® real semi sweet chocolate chips**
**25 squares (about 6 ounces) Choceur® white chocolate, chopped**
**1 teaspoon peppermint extract**
**20 squares (about 6 ounces) Choceur® milk chocolate, chopped**

1. Line 8-inch square pan with Kwik-N-Fresh® aluminum foil, leaving 1-inch overhang on sides.

2. Place chocolate chips in top of double boiler over simmering water. Stir until melted. Remove from heat. Spread melted chocolate onto bottom of prepared pan. Let stand until firm. (If not firm after 45 minutes, refrigerate 10 minutes.)

3. Melt white chocolate in clean double boiler; stir in peppermint extract. Spread over chocolate layer. Shake pan to spread evenly. Let stand 45 minutes or until set.

4. Melt milk chocolate in same double boiler. Spread over white chocolate layer. Shake pan to spread evenly. Let stand 45 minutes or until set.

5. Cut mints into 16 (2-inch) squares. Remove from pan by lifting mints and foil with foil handles. Place squares on cutting board. Cut each square diagonally into 2 triangles. Cut in half again to make 64 small triangles. Store in airtight container in refrigerator.

*Makes 64 mints*

# Moist Pumpkin Cookies

2¼ cups Grandma's Best® all-purpose flour
1¼ teaspoons ground cinnamon
  1 teaspoon Baker's Corner® baking powder
  ½ teaspoon Baker's Corner® baking soda
  ½ teaspoon Sebree® salt
  ½ teaspoon ground nutmeg
  ½ cup (1 stick) Happy Farms® butter, softened
  1 cup Sweet Harvest® packed light brown sugar
  ½ cup Sweet Harvest® granulated sugar
1½ cups Sweet Harvest® solid pack pumpkin
  1 Goldhen® egg
  1 teaspoon Spice Club vanilla
  ¾ cup Sweet Harvest® raisins
  ½ cup Southern Grove® chopped walnuts
    Powdered Sugar Glaze (recipe follows)

1. Preheat oven to 350°F. Combine flour, cinnamon, baking powder, baking soda, salt and nutmeg in small bowl; set aside.

2. Beat butter and sugars in large bowl until creamy. Beat in pumpkin, egg and vanilla until light and fluffy. Stir in flour mixture until well blended. Stir in raisins and walnuts. Drop heaping tablespoonfuls of dough 2 inches apart onto ungreased cookie sheets.

3. Bake 12 to 15 minutes or until set. Cool 2 minutes on cookie sheets. Remove to wire racks; cool completely. Prepare Powdered Sugar Glaze. Drizzle glaze over cookies. Let glaze set. Store between layers of waxed paper in airtight containers.

*Makes about 3 dozen cookies*

Powdered Sugar Glaze: Combine 1 cup Sweet Harvest® powdered sugar and 2 tablespoons Friendly Farms® milk in small bowl until well blended.

## HOLIDAY TIP

*Holiday cookies make great gifts for friends and family near and far. When shipping cookies, choose soft, moist cookies. They will survive shipping better than fragile, crisp ones. Wrap each flavor of cookie separately to retain flavors and textures.*

# Gem of a Snowman Glass Container

## supplies

- 4-inch round glass jar with metal push-on lid
- 16-ounce package clear glass gems
- Polished river pebbles: orange or yellow tones and black
- Hot glue gun and glue sticks
- ⅛ yard plaid fabric
- Ruler
- Scissors
- Evergreen sprig

## tip

Before you begin, wash jar and lid to remove any oils from glass surface. For best results, hot glue flat side of clear glass gems to jar. This will provide more surface contact and ensure a better hold.

1. Remove lid and set aside. Working from front bottom edge of jar up, glue glass gems and pebbles to jar to create snowman's face. For nose, hot glue 1 glass gem upside down onto jar so pebble can be adhered to flat side of gem. Leave room at top of jar (about 1 to 1½ inches) for lid and fabric bow. Continue gluing glass gems to cover entire jar.

2. Cut small slit ½ inch from raw edge of fabric. Grip on either side of slit and tear down entire length. Discard torn ½-inch strip. Cut a second slit 1½ inches from torn edge of remaining fabric. Tear again to create strip that is torn on both side of edges. Wrap strip around top of jar. Tie ends into bow. Trim excess fabric. Insert evergreen sprig behind bow. Replace lid.

ALDI

# METRIC CONVERSION CHART

### VOLUME MEASUREMENTS (dry)

1/8 teaspoon = 0.5 mL
1/4 teaspoon = 1 mL
1/2 teaspoon = 2 mL
3/4 teaspoon = 4 mL
1 teaspoon = 5 mL
1 tablespoon = 15 mL
2 tablespoons = 30 mL
1/4 cup = 60 mL
1/3 cup = 75 mL
1/2 cup = 125 mL
2/3 cup = 150 mL
3/4 cup = 175 mL
1 cup = 250 mL
2 cups = 1 pint = 500 mL
3 cups = 750 mL
4 cups = 1 quart = 1 L

### VOLUME MEASUREMENTS (fluid)

1 fluid ounce (2 tablespoons) = 30 mL
4 fluid ounces (1/2 cup) = 125 mL
8 fluid ounces (1 cup) = 250 mL
12 fluid ounces (1 1/2 cups) = 375 mL
16 fluid ounces (2 cups) = 500 mL

### WEIGHTS (mass)

1/2 ounce = 15 g
1 ounce = 30 g
3 ounces = 90 g
4 ounces = 120 g
8 ounces = 225 g
10 ounces = 285 g
12 ounces = 360 g
16 ounces = 1 pound = 450 g

### DIMENSIONS

1/16 inch = 2 mm
1/8 inch = 3 mm
1/4 inch = 6 mm
1/2 inch = 1.5 cm
3/4 inch = 2 cm
1 inch = 2.5 cm

### OVEN TEMPERATURES

250°F = 120°C
275°F = 140°C
300°F = 150°C
325°F = 160°C
350°F = 180°C
375°F = 190°C
400°F = 200°C
425°F = 220°C
450°F = 230°C

### BAKING PAN SIZES

| Utensil | Size in Inches/Quarts | Metric Volume | Size in Centimeters |
|---|---|---|---|
| Baking or Cake Pan (square or rectangular) | 8×8×2 | 2 L | 20×20×5 |
| | 9×9×2 | 2.5 L | 23×23×5 |
| | 12×8×2 | 3 L | 30×20×5 |
| | 13×9×2 | 3.5 L | 33×23×5 |
| Loaf Pan | 8×4×3 | 1.5 L | 20×10×7 |
| | 9×5×3 | 2 L | 23×13×7 |
| Round Layer Cake Pan | 8×1½ | 1.2 L | 20×4 |
| | 9×1½ | 1.5 L | 23×4 |
| Pie Plate | 8×1¼ | 750 mL | 20×3 |
| | 9×1¼ | 1 L | 23×3 |
| Baking Dish or Casserole | 1 quart | 1 L | — |
| | 1½ quart | 1.5 L | — |
| | 2 quart | 2 L | — |